D0457836

DECEIVED BY THE NEW AGE

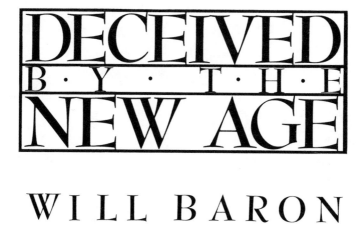

DECEIVED B·Y·T·H·E NEW AGE

WILL BARON

Pacific Press Publishing Association
Boise, Idaho
Oshawa, Ontario, Canada

Unless otherwise indicated, Scripture quotations are taken from the New International Version.

All people in this story are real characters. Some names have been changed to protect privacy.

Edited by Bonnie Widicker
Designed by Linda Griffith
Cover illustration by Bryant Eastman
Typeset in 10/12 Bookman

Copyright © 1990 by
Alexander W. Baron
Printed in United States of America
All Rights Reserved

Library of Congress Catalog Card Number: 89-62157

ISBN 0-8163-0878-0

90 91 92 93 94 • 5 4 3 2

Contents

Introduction

There is something intriguing about the scene. With the tranquil blue Pacific Ocean rolling gently in the background, the young evangelist is standing on the green lawn and boldly preaches to a group of curious listeners. In excitement, the man tells his audience about the soon return of Jesus Christ, having attracted their attention by the large picture of Jesus displayed beside him. To all intents and purposes, he appears to be a zealous Christian working for the cause of the gospel.

However, if you made an investigation into the background of this beach evangelist, you would gasp in astonishment. You would discover that he was not a real Christian at all, but was, in fact, an occultist, a member of the New Age movement, a person controlled by the powers of darkness.

In bewilderment, you would ask, What is a devout New Ager doing, preaching to strangers about the soon coming of Jesus? Why does he spend each weekend carrying out a solitary outdoor ministry that appears to promote Christianity? Who is this man, and how did he become involved in his strange activities?

The mysterious beach evangelist was Will Baron. His story is going to take you into the bizarre world of the

7

Mastermind and his evil New Age conspiracy.

Will spent twelve years of his life in dedicated involvement with the New Age movement. He shudders as he recalls how he was seduced into becoming part of a secret invasion force of counterfeit Christians. As he subtly introduced his listeners to New Age concepts packaged in Christian terminology, he sincerely believed he was working for the Jesus Christ of the Bible. Even some pastors regarded him to be a follower of Christ.

Like Shirley MacLaine and other cultists, Will really thought he was trying to lead people into a closer relationship with God. He had never heard of the Mastermind.

The Mastermind's agents may have infiltrated into your own church, and you are not aware of who they are. They are not easy to recognize because they seem to talk and behave like normal Christians.

Today, Will is a true Christian. As a result of earnest prayers by family members who suspected he had been led astray into cultic darkness, the Holy Spirit orchestrated a dramatic rescue from the intricate web of deception that had enmeshed him.

His incredible experience reveals the deceptive workings of the New Age master plan to infiltrate the body of Christ. The grand finale of the plan is predicted to be the appearance of the Antichrist in the church amidst a display of incredible signs, wonders, and miracles. From bitter experience, Will regards the deception to be far more powerful and dangerous than most people realize. For example, prior to his involvement in the New Age, Will wasn't an atheist or someone ignorant of the biblical gospel. He was actually brought up by devout Christian parents and regularly attended church until he was twenty-four years old.

You will be amazed at his true story.

Chapter 1

The New Age Enticement of Christians

"Get down on your knees!"

"Get down on your knees. I am Jesus Christ, and I am going to heal you."

I listened to Muriel's narrative with fascination. She was standing at the front of the class in our New Age center and was describing an incredible experience that had recently occurred to her in the middle of the night.

"I am telling you the truth," Muriel continued with excitement. "He stood there right in the middle of my locked bedroom and told me to get down on my knees. If people think that Jesus is a weedy weakling, they are in for a big surprise. He is over six feet tall and looks very dignified and handsome.

"He is a power-r-r-ful being," she stressed with force.

I started to feel somewhat uneasy as I sat listening to Muriel's account. Blonde and of good height, she was about sixty years old and looked fairly slender in her attractive blue dress. Her face beaming with joy, the founder and director of our center described what happened next.

"I got out of bed and knelt in front of Jesus. He laid his hands upon my head and gave me a blessing. Then he turned around and walked straight through the solid, locked door of my hotel room."

9

Muriel commented matter-of-factly, "He was gone. He just disappeared into the corridor."

This was the second occasion in which I had listened to Muriel's account of the visit by Jesus to her hotel room. After her experience, many changes started taking place in the Lighted Way, our small metaphysical organization. I was becoming quite confused. The new Christian emphasis made me feel uncomfortable.

It wasn't that I disbelieved Muriel's experience. On the contrary, I fully accepted her narrative as being factual. After all, I was a board member of the center and had known Muriel for several years. She was very spiritual, and I had never observed her to lie or exaggerate. What made me feel uneasy was the new focus upon the Bible.

Muriel was a New Age channeler, or spirit medium,* when she founded the Lighted Way in the early sixties. Shortly after her visit from Jesus in 1985, she communicated a message from the Holy Spirit saying that I should throw away all my occult books and start to study the Bible instead. I was reluctant to accept her advice and give up my beloved esoteric volumes.

I had been a member of the Lighted Way for five years and loved the metaphysical teachings. Over the years I had had many spiritual experiences, some of them as important to me personally as Muriel's visit from Jesus was to her. For example, about a year after my first visit to the Lighted Way, I became a devotee of a noted Hindu/Buddhist guru called Djwhal Khul. After the four-year relationship with Djwhal Khul, I could not understand why I should suddenly become a follower of Jesus Christ instead and be required to trash all my occult books!

---

*Channelers are New Age mediums who claim to be able to receive messages from intelligent spirit entities existing in the spirit realms. The act of channeling is the verbalization by the medium of any messages received.

Muriel had stated that the metaphysical books were only half-truths and that the Bible was a much greater source of divine wisdom. But I remained reluctant to become involved in this Christianity.

I gradually began to acknowledge the fact that Jesus had taken over our center and that I must accept him as my master. I purchased a Bible and started to attend the weekly Bible-study classes and prayer groups that were being offered in lieu of classes on metaphysics.

The teachings expounded at the Lighted Way evolved into a curious mixture of New Age mysticism and biblical Christianity. We regarded ourselves as New Age Christians. I even began to tell people that I was a born-again Christian. After all, I had given up my Hindu guru and accepted "Jesus Christ" as my master and saviour.

During my meditation periods, I could sense that "Jesus Christ" and the "Holy Spirit" were inspiring me through my voice of conscience, exactly in the manner that Djwhal Khul seemed to have done previously. After a while, I became devoted to this Jesus. He took over my life.

I was also told to attend regular Christian church congregations so that I could meet new friends and interest them in meditation and other less offensive New Age ideas disguised in biblical-sounding terms.

Avoiding anything too controversial, I presented subtle suggestions here and there. I found quite a few people who were willing to listen to my interesting proposals. For example, a pastor from an evangelical congregation told me it would be a good idea for me to start a meditation group in his church if I could get some people interested.

Two years after the mysterious visit by "Jesus Christ" to the director of our New Age center, I experienced a dramatic conversion to authentic Christianity and discovered that the Jesus Christ I was following was not the real Jesus, Son of God Almighty. I was devastated to learn that as a New Age Christian, I had been following false prophets and false teachings purporting to be revelations of wisdom from God.

You may be wondering, Who or what appeared to Muriel in her hotel room? Was it her imagination? Or was it perhaps a demon in a disguise, pretending to be Jesus?

Regarding the second possibility, perhaps you do not believe in the existence of satanic angels. When I was a Christian youth, I held the same view. Believing that evil angels were simply mythical, I never thought it was possible to be influenced by them. However, some definite power certainly took control of our center and my personal life. I was destined to have a profound and incredible learning experience before I was pulled from the clutches of darkness and brought into the true light of a relationship with Christ.

The New Age Seduction of Christians

Several months after my rescue from the New Age and its counterfeit Christianity arm, I gave a personal testimony about my experiences to a large group of Christians at a camp meeting. I told them about my experience of being held firmly in the grip of deception perpetrated by the New Age cult movement and about its endeavor to fuse Eastern philosophy with Christianity.

After the talk, a middle-aged Christian couple approached me. With a worried expression on his face, the father reported: "Our daughter was always rather timid and nervous. She recently started to attend Yoga classes. Now she is also doing meditation in order to find peace and relaxation. She tells us that it works. She is becoming more and more interested in other New Age ideas and will not listen to anything we tell her. She still sings in our church choir. What can we do?"

Maybe you have an acquaintance involved in the New Age. I have discovered that it is subtly luring many Christians into its influence. As a teenager, I, too, was one of the victims. Even though I had been brought up in a Christian family that attended church each week, I was still deceived by the New Age movement's promises of health, happiness, and fulfillment. I was completely led astray, eventually becoming totally immersed in the world of the occult. It really can happen to anyone—you, your family, or your friends.

For example, my own active involvement with the New Age movement began when I joined a London-based international networking organization called Health for the New Age. Not even knowing what the term "New Age" meant, I wasn't looking for spirit guides or occult practices. I was simply interested in finding information about alternative healing techniques for a condition that I had. My innocent interest eventually led me onto the path of obedience to the powers of deception. Apparently, my Christian upbringing failed to give me the knowledge that would have alerted me to the dangers of the course I was taking.

Knowledge, success, and oneness with "God" are the promises the New Age movement presents to the potential victims it is about to ensnare. And thousands of unsuspecting individuals—Christians and atheists alike—are swallowing this lure. Many orthodox Christians, including some pastors, have tasted the New Age bait and found that it "was good for food and pleasing to the eye, and also desirable for gaining wisdom" (Genesis 3:6).

During the time I was a New Age Christian, it was very pleasing to find that a few Christian preachers were already teaching some of the New Age beliefs. Joyfully hearing them express statements that were in line with what I had learned in my metaphysical training, I reasoned that these preachers must have received revelation knowledge directly from the spirit realm, or possibly were inspired by the New Age writings in widespread circulation. Your own pastor may have expressed odd interpretations of biblical passages, and you are not quite sure where he is coming from.

The New Age teachings and practices have now become so widespread that most Christians are quite likely to come into contact with them in one form or another. Often people are not aware of that exposure. For example, maybe you have been to healing professionals who practice new and interesting techniques, and you were unaware those techniques are New Age oriented.

Like Nancy Reagan, perhaps someone in your family has taken an interest in astrology, thinking that it may be beneficial, or, at worst, just harmless fun. I am sure the wife of our popular former President did not realize that astrology is an ancient divination practice originating from pagan Babylon and is expressly forbidden by the Bible.

It is possible you may have sought advice from a psychological counselor, and, unknown to you, he was a New Ager, and you were being exposed to a subtle web of evil deceit.

If you have desired to seek closeness with God, perhaps meditation has attracted your attention, that so-called science of seeking communion with God. You may have wondered whether it is really a good idea for a Christian to meditate.

I first began to practice New Age introspective meditation in a class at the Lighted Way metaphysical center. Some people begin New Age meditation techniques right in their own churches. Like my acquaintance Jean, for example. She is a secretary with a large Christian publishing house. As she sat at her desk reading through one of my manuscripts, several questions started to surface concerning her own recent activity.

Jean reported: "I am going to a Bible study in which the teacher asks the members of the class to sit quietly and try to listen for God's voice. I wonder if this is the beginning of what you talk about in the book."

"You bet it is," was my reply. "It sounds to me like a classic case of the invasion of New Age techniques right

into your own church. This type of introspective meditation is not found in the Bible, and it has never been part
of orthodox Christian activity. It is a Hindu practice that
is undesirable and potentially dangerous!"

Occultist Lectures in Methodist Church

Some churches in my own area *openly* accommodate
New Agers and their evil philosophies. Take, for example,
a large Methodist church in the Los Angeles area. It has
boldly rented its sanctuary to the renowned New Age
celebrity Benjamin Creme so that he could present his
West Coast lectures on the subject of the second coming
of "the Christ" to planet Earth. Creme is an occultist who
placed full-page advertisements in eighteen of the world's
major newspapers in 1982, announcing that "the Christ"
had returned and was living in London.

Jesus warned that Creme's type of activity will happen toward the end of the age:

> At that time if anyone says to you, "Look, here
> is the Christ!" or, "There he is!" do not believe it.
> For false Christs and false prophets will appear
> and perform great signs and miracles to deceive
> even the elect—if that were possible. See, I have
> told you ahead of time (Matthew 24:23-25).

Note that even the elect are in danger of being
deceived. I hope your pastor would not rent your church
to an agent of the Antichrist conspiracy.

Are New Age Philosophies Really That Bad?

Initially, I felt grateful that I had been led into the New
Age movement. The teachings answered many questions
and gave hope for the future. The New Age appeared to
offer everything that I had been looking for. I felt part of a
movement, part of a group of people who were genuinely
seeking to improve the quality of life on this planet and
who were seeking to harmonize their lives with God.

I came to believe that if I applied the New Age teachings and techniques in my life, my skills and talents would develop to their full potential, and I would attain fulfillment and happiness.

For example, I began to practice meditation in the hope of receiving enlightenment. In meditation, I became aware that it was possible to tune in to an inner voice of conscience that seemed to give wise advice. Known by New Agers as the voice of the "higher self," it was not some strange voice speaking to me, but was more like my own voice of conscience—with a special clarity and composure—speaking to me in a new and distinct manner. The newly found conscience seemed to operate from a higher level of wisdom than my regular, logical thoughts. The New Agers regard this inner voice as an expression of the voice of God, a manifestation of the Holy Spirit as it speaks through the mind. I was delighted to discover this source of "divine" wisdom within my own mind as it prompted me to make many beneficial changes in my life.

Unfortunately, after the first few years of apparent blessings, life gradually became a nightmare of slavery to the dictates coming from my perverted inner voice of conscience. For example, my endeavors to secure the financial prosperity promised by the New Age prophets resulted in monetary debt as I was forced by my conscience to make large donations to help finance the operations of the Lighted Way and its advertising thrusts to promote New Age "Christianity." Any disobedience began to result in severe depression, which I perceived to be the feeling of separation from "God" because I was disobedient to his will. As soon as I donated the amount of money I had been commanded to give, the intense depression lifted immediately. This scenario occurred repeatedly; like a puppet on a string, I was being controlled by a strange and awesome force.

The cult of the New Age is similar to all other cults. It doesn't matter whether you are a slave to false voices of conscience, to spirit guides, or to cult organization leaders; the process of intimidation, guilt, and bondage is very similar. However, the progressive deception was so subtle that I never suspected I was being manipulated by some kind of evil power.

A Promise of Immortality

It became my hope that New Age Christianity would bring me into immortality, the eternal life promised by Christ. I was unaware that Satan was using New Age teaching to perpetuate the lie he told Eve in the garden: "You will not surely die" (Genesis 3:4). Believing this lie, I had to accept distorted interpretations of the clear scriptural statements that "death came to all men, because all sinned" (Romans 5:12) and that the wages of sin is death (see Romans 6:23).

I had believed that all the different avenues of religious expression would ultimately lead to God, whether those expressions were colored by Hinduism, Buddhism, or something else. The idea that all spiritual paths lead to God is one of the fundamental New Age doctrines.

But the Bible says something different:

Wide is the gate and broad is the road that leads to destruction, and many enter through it. But small is the gate and narrow the road that leads to life, and only a few find it (Matthew 7:13, 14).

Upon my rescue from the New Age, I was stunned to realize that even though I was praying and preaching in the name of Jesus, in reality I was traveling the wide road to destruction. Perhaps you think it is impossible for someone to be preaching and praying in the name of Jesus while being under the control of the powers of darkness.

Christ warned that there would arise false teachers

who would preach *in his name*:

> Many will say to me on that day, "Lord, Lord, did we not prophesy in your name, and in your name drive out demons and perform many miracles?" Then I will tell them plainly, "I never knew you. Away from me, you evildoers!" (Matthew 7:22, 23).

You need to know about my former activities because right now others are doing exactly what I was doing. You need to be able to recognize them before they lead you or your church astray into false doctrines and questionable practices.

Before I describe how I was seduced by the Mastermind, I would like to tell you a little about my background.

The Disappearance of God

I was born thirty-nine years ago into a Christian family who methodically attended church each week. My father was a lay preacher in the small congregation. Even though I believed that Jesus was the Son of God, I gradually developed an attitude of apathy and coldness toward Christianity.

I think much of this attitude can be attributed to the neighborhood in which I grew up—a medium-sized town located in the industrial region of northern England. Factory chimneys endlessly belched out smoke into the drab, cloudy sky. People seemed oriented to a secular, coarse lifestyle. Among my friends, religion was hardly ever talked about except as a subject for rude jokes and as a means of expressing profanities. Schoolteachers never mentioned God, and everyone seemed to get along fine without religion.

I began to drift into the worldly values and activities of my friends. At first it was small things, such as minor vandalism, smoking, and stealing liquor from my uncle's pantry. More serious was the tendency never to think about God or Jesus or about the role they should have in my life.

As I became more involved with my predominantly ungodly friends, I gradually categorized religion as something that belonged to my parents, but not to me. Even though I believed that Jesus had existed as the Bible teaches, I felt no special relationship with him. And yet, surprisingly, I felt secure that if I died I would go to heaven.

My alienation from Christian values intensified in high school, where my teachers exposed me to fascinating ideas such as the theories of evolution, reincarnation, and extrasensory perception.

I recall one teacher in particular. Mr. Harding looked to be in his early thirties. He was of medium height and build, with reddish-brown hair neatly styled in a manner typical of British high-school teachers. But he seemed to be different from most schoolmasters. A rather solitary character, he often could be seen in his beige raincoat sitting by himself in local cafes. Even though I was a sciences student, I found his twice-weekly philosophy class to be most interesting.

"Freud says" was one of Mr. Harding's most common phrases as he introduced us to the ideas of Sigmund Freud, the famous psychoanalyst.

"Freud says that man's unconscious mind is a very powerful force in his life," commented Mr. Harding. "He believed that all the idiosyncrasies in our motives and emotions result from the workings of the unconscious."

I had a deep personal interest in Mr. Harding's statements. Sitting in his class, or in any of my high-school classes, for that matter, I often felt discomforting anxieties and fears. Sometimes my chest would tighten, and a dark wave of claustrophobia would descend upon me like a nightmare, giving me the powerful urge to leave the room, for no apparent reason. I knew the feeling was irrational, but could not understand my fearful response.

The problem had started one morning when I was sixteen years old. During a school assembly in the auditorium, I was suddenly overwhelmed by a panic attack. I had felt tension and stress building inside of me for months. On this particular morning, the tension seemed to explode in an attack of fear and anxiety, which I had difficulty keeping under control. My chest tightened as if a steel band had been wrapped around it, and I thought I was going to faint from lack of oxygen. It seemed as if I were under a cloud of impending doom as I wrestled to keep my thinking clear. Using every drop of willpower available, I fought the urge to run and forced myself to stay outwardly composed until the assembly was over.

After this first panic attack, I was never again the same person. My late teens seemed to be dogged with incessant anxiety. The family doctor prescribed tranquilizers and told me to take it easy. I was disappointed when he failed to give any meaningful reasons for my condition.

"Why do I feel this way?" I asked him.

"I think you may have been working too hard," he suggested nonchalantly. His vagueness precipitated a lack of confidence in his diagnosis. To be truthful, excessive study did make me feel worse, but I could not agree that it was the basic cause of my condition. I intuitively sensed that something had changed inside my nervous system as I became an adolescent, but I did not know what to do to correct the condition.

While listening to Mr. Harding's Freudian-oriented philosophy talks, I wondered whether the anxiety was connected with my unconscious mind, as proposed in Freud's psychology theories. Perhaps Freud's books could throw some light upon my strange feelings of tension and alienation.

Being motivated to read some of Freud's works, I began to evolve a general opinion that all human problems could be explained in terms of dysfunctions associated with the unconscious mind. I thought, Perhaps religion itself is a neurosis, a condition of psychological weakness, a mask for an underlying lack of maturity. This was a view that Freud expounded.

This led me to question whether Satan really existed. Were temptations really a process of some evil being playing psychic war games with his victim, as the church taught? Freud expressed the contrasting idea that the activity of the subconscious mind was responsible for conflicting thoughts and impulses. He believed that a person's irrational and antisocial actions were highly influenced by the unconscious memories associated with detrimental childhood experiences called trauma.

I began to agree with Freud's view and regarded Satan as a purely mythical symbolic representation of man's inner disordered state with its destructive impulses. To deal with this condition, one needed greater psychological understanding.

After digesting a couple of Freud's books, I focused my efforts once again upon academic studies. My fear and anxiety had abated somewhat, and my interest in psychology waned. However, Freud's ideas had deeply affected my attitude toward religion.

"Will, are you going to the fresher's stag night this evening?" Brian asked as he took off his black-framed spectacles in the elevator. A friendly guy of rather thin build, Brian was a fellow university freshman living on the same floor of our students' accommodation building. It was my first week of beginning a bachelor's course in physics.

"What is a stag night?" I asked with curiosity, having never lived in a big city before.

"Oh, it's a striptease show with plenty of booze. The students' union has organized a special show for all the freshmen. Why don't you come with us?"

I knew it wouldn't be the right thing to do. But even though I wasn't really too interested in the suggestion, I felt as if I could just do with some kind of excitement to pass the evening and get away from the worries and stress of starting university life.

"I guess I'll come with you. Sounds like it may be fun," I said with a lump in my throat. As a student at a university, I wanted to stretch my boundaries to see what kinds of things were happening in the bright lights of the metropolitan city of Manchester. In a spirit of rebelliousness, I didn't want anything to stop me from having a "good time," especially not my conscience.

Out of curiosity, a few weeks later I visited pornographic movie theaters on a couple of occasions. They were a terrible bore, but at least I felt I was exercising my initiative and maturity to search for some excitement to break the loneliness of student life.

The university's bars and weekend rock shows now attracted my attention. However, even they became boring unless I had a couple of beers to help me loosen up a little. As intoxication progressed, my lowered moral standards enabled me to amuse Brian and our companions by telling lewd jokes, much to their cheering applause.

What relationship I may have had with Christ was now over, even though my "body" still attended church once a week so that things would look good in our family. Like a kind of Jekyll and Hyde, I became a double personality, putting on an air of respectability in church, but living an unchristian life outside of it.

Upon leaving the university, I aspired to find fulfillment in a career and in the pursuit of leisure. Becoming an engineering designer-draughtsman for a large manufacturer of textile machinery, I was busy earning and spending money, trying to satisfy an insatiable thirst for excitement through motorcycles, cars, travel, partying, and bars.

When I was about twenty-four years old, I decided to quit the token visits to church, even though I was afraid my family would treat me as an outcast. It was not easy to leave the church. Quite frankly, I was afraid that the Christian gospel might be true after all, and my life would end in damnation. After weeks of excruciating deliberation, I finally decided to cease all church attendance. I rationalized that I would "take a vacation" from all religion for a while to see how I would feel. Then perhaps later I would reassess my beliefs.

Life without any religion seemed to be better than the former pretense—at least now my beliefs and behavior were consistent. For example, I noticed I could now use profanities and pornographic expressions without arousing any nudge from my conscience, leaving me completely free to do as I pleased.

"Eat, drink, and be merry, for tomorrow we die" became an apt symbolism for my life. But a new problem developed. I didn't die, and it was getting more and more difficult to be merry, no matter how active my social life became. And frantically active it had become: the once withdrawn high-school student was now involved in anything from motorcycle gangs to mountaineering, from shady bars to rock festivals. However, after playing out these activities, the old feeling of unfulfillment would creep upon me.

A letter arrived from my older sister. "Why don't you come and live with us in Canada?" she wrote. "You can start a whole new life in this land of opportunity." My sister had emigrated to Toronto with her husband and family several years before. The invitation sounded appealing.

Deciding I needed some drastic change to get out of my rut, I took her advice and flew out to a prospective new life. Unfortunately, being in a new country did not seem to alter the way I felt. I also very much missed my friends back in England. After a few months, I returned to my hometown.

I now became more acutely aware of the underlying unfulfillment and creeping depression. Further, the phobias and tension I had felt in my teens had never completely left me, and I wanted so much to feel relaxed and completely at ease. Remembering my high-school teacher's high esteem for Freud, I decided to turn to psychology as a means of finding answers to the problems of my life.

Paying many visits to a local lending library, I borrowed several books on psychology. In my thinking, I wondered, Could a correct application of this psychology give me peace and contentment in life? The ideas expressed in the pages sounded very promising.

One small book on the library shelf caught my special attention.

Chapter 2

Seduced by Psychic Power

A strong-looking man with a full head of black, wavy hair, psychotherapist Peter Blythe completely changed my life. But I have never met him.

No, he did not give me counseling over the phone. In fact, he is unaware of his incredible effect on my life, for he has never been acquainted with me. I know how he looks only from a picture on the back cover of his small book *Stress Disease*.

I will never forget the title. It sounded innocent enough as I pulled the little volume from a library shelf. Have you ever read something that totally altered your life? *Stress Disease* stimulated a series of changes that resulted in my switching careers, living on a different continent, and becoming fully immersed in a satanic cult. The power of a book can be phenomenal.

Initially, Peter Blythe's book seemed to offer me hope that I could understand my feelings of fear and alienation. Perhaps I could find a solution for my recurrent claustrophobia, which, although mild at this time, was still bothersome.

In looking for healing, meaning, and harmony in my life, the first part of *Stress Disease* appeared to offer interesting insights regarding my problems. The book then progressed into an eclectic discussion of the cause and cure of disease in general. It introduced the New

Age "holistic" concept, the idea that body, mind, and spirit are inseparable, and that each needs to be in harmony in order to produce total health.

The idea of "holistic health" sounded appealing. The concept of a necessary balance between body, mind, and spirit made sense. I thought, Maybe I can pick up some good advice and pass it on to my friends.

The last few chapters presented information on "alternative therapy" techniques for common diseases. Being familiar only with surgery and medication, I was fascinated to read of therapies such as acupuncture, homeopathy, psychic surgery, chakra balancing, rebirthing, primal therapy, reiki, crystals, and bioenergetics. Descriptions of these treatments talked a lot about "energies," "balance," and "wholeness."

It was the first time I had ever heard of the term "New Age." I had no idea what it meant. I wasn't interested in getting involved in the occult; I was simply searching for better health and for contentment.

Stress Disease mentioned a London-based organization called Health for the New Age. Wanting to learn more about these alternative healing practices, I joined it and arranged to have a meeting with its founder.

The New Shamanism

Colonel Marcus McCausland was sitting in a chair directly in front of me. He epitomized the typical retired British army officer. Dressed in a tweed sports jacket, he was tall, with a medium build. His gait was as erect as a marine sentry's.

"I am impressed with your knowledge and ideas," he told me, referring to our conversation. He, his wife, and I were sitting in their home, discussing the latest psychology theories in circulation. The purpose of my visit was to obtain their opinions regarding the new psychology ideas being introduced into Britain from America. Marcus was the director of Health for the New Age, the organization that I had recently joined. His speech was kind and considerate, yet retained the firmness of his military background.

"Well, I have still a lot more to learn," I assured my hosts, modestly responding to their praise.

Their organization acted as an international networking agency for collecting and sharing data on New Age–oriented "alternative" therapies. One of Marcus's special interests was research and treatment for cancer.

"Marcus, I am sure Will has known all his ideas before coming into his present life," commented Mrs. McCausland as she lifted up her arms to stretch. This statement, made by an attractive, highly educated woman, caught me by surprise.

"Are you suggesting I have lived before?" I asked doubtfully.

"Oh, yes. I am sure of that," replied Marcus as if expressing a military fact. "We have all lived many lives. I am certain a lot of your insights concerning psychology have been brought with you from your previous life."

"Will," interrupted Mrs. McCausland, "you are now simply relearning what you have already known."

I was speechless. Although I had previously considered the idea of reincarnation, I had never met anyone who had spoken about past lives with such frankness. Because Marcus's wife was a respected professional psychologist, I felt quite open to seriously accepting her revealing statement. You know how it is; one tends to trust qualified people.

I left the McCauslands' home with a sense of excitement and interest regarding my past lives and a renewed optimism about my potential for success in this life.

My subsequent seduction into the New Age movement was a gradual process. Over the next couple of years I had contact with more New Age followers and digested more and more literature expounding their ideas. Being seduced into the New Age through an original interest in alternative healing techniques seems to be a common occurrence. In fact, it appears to be one of the main methods of recruitment used by the New Age devotees. Many of them offer therapy and counseling to people in need—and then interest their clients in the philosophies associated with their practices. Often people with serious medical conditions are drawn to New Age healing methods—a potentially deceptive arena.

As a searcher for answers from the field of psychology, I never expected that my quest for meaning in life would bring me into the sphere of false religions and their evil practices.

From Psychology to Mysticism

While retaining a casual interest in New Age philosophy, I mainly desired to eliminate the anxieties that plagued me. If I could achieve a sense of inner peace, I felt I would be able to develop my career potential and enhance my personal relationships. As a result of the information in Peter Blythe's little book, for a couple of years I became involved in such activities as personal counseling, encounter groups, human potential seminars, and group process workshops. However, England provided only limited access to such information. From what I had read, Los Angeles seemed a much better place to experience that sort of thing, so I decided to move there at the end of the seventies.

My involvement with the Los Angeles psychology and growth movement proved beneficial at first. But after about a year, I became disillusioned when a psychology center I attended closed down due to a lack of harmony between its founders. I began to wonder about the spiritual or mystical aspects of my life that the book *Stress Disease* had indicated needed to be in harmony.

I recall feeling lost and quite depressed in the engineering office at work one day. I just didn't know what I should do with my life. As I was making some copies of machinery drawings, I distinctly heard a voice deep inside my mind. "What about your soul?" it asked.

It was as if a clear and profound voice of conscience spoke to me. Being confronted by these words made me feel very uncomfortable, as if the lingering emptiness inside of me had been exposed wide open.

Under the influence of secular psychology, I was continuing to live an ungodly lifestyle. Wondering what this voice meant by *soul*, I asked myself, Is this the voice of God prompting me to return to Christianity? Does my soul need saving from damnation?

Having learned that regular psychologists have limited skills and abilities in understanding the spiritual dimension of human motives and experience, I was reluctant to turn to them for illumination. They always sounded good; they always looked good when lecturing, but their ideas and advice often tended to have limited effect once one had made the necessary adjustments to correct the more serious weaknesses of one's personality. After one had made beneficial behavior and lifestyle changes, further consultation with psychologists sometimes seemed to provide nothing more than human contact. Good friends should provide this support, if you have them.

Although the inner voice used the word *soul*, I did not want to be involved with any kind of formal religion, such as Christianity. Instead, I was drawn deeper into the New Age.

Precipitated in part by my interest in past lives, I was impressed to search for someone with special ability who could give me counseling regarding my destiny. I wanted to meet someone like a shaman—a person with special power, wisdom, and knowledge; a person with profound psychic abilities, able to probe into the deepest depths of my psyche. I aspired to consult with someone who could tell me exactly what I needed to do in order to fulfill my destiny potential for this lifetime. I wanted to find someone who could tell me about my soul, that part of me that the mysterious voice of conscience had brought to my attention. Perhaps, I thought, I can find this kind of wise counselor in a Los Angeles New Age organization.

New Age Prophets and Their Psychic Power

The advertisement caught my attention in a peculiar way. It was as if something deep inside me responded with a subtle prompting to attend the psychic fair listed in a New Age magazine I was looking through. I thought to myself, Perhaps this psychic fair is a good place to start my search for someone with power to point me to my destiny.

The event was listed as being held at a metaphysical center called the Lighted Way. Concerned that psychics might be a bunch of frauds, I planned to check out the center first. If I had a good feeling about the place, I would inquire about the possibility of having an in-depth, private, psychic counseling session. It was not my desire to have a cheap, quick reading with an amateur fortuneteller; I was on a serious mission looking for someone special.

On the day of the fair, I drove over to the affluent Los Angeles suburb of Pacific Palisades, where the Lighted Way was located in a beautiful commercial building in the Palisades Highlands, a picturesque valley deep in the Santa Monica Mountains. Having never been to a psychic fair before, I had no idea what to expect.

My entrance into the metaphysical center was heralded by the sound of Tibetan chimes gently clinking and clanging as I brushed past the opened door. The chimes seemed to be welcoming me into the new and enchanting world of Eastern mysticism.

Shelves of neatly displayed books lined the walls of the first room. As I walked through the book area and entered the main room, my eyes were attracted to the floor. It was covered with a most beautiful shimmering, light green carpet. With its fluorescent glow, it seemed to draw me into the room.

I felt a strange sense of peace in the place, a peculiar,

intriguing atmosphere. Inhaling deeply, I noticed the sweet aroma of incense. It seemed to give the room a sacred feeling.

Evenly spaced in the large room were four psychic readers, each seated at an individual table. One or two clients were consulting with the readers. I hurriedly scanned the scene, for I did not want anyone to notice that I was unfamiliar with what was occurring in the room.

Behind the reception counter stood a middle-aged woman of medium height and slim build wearing a dress with a pretty floral pattern. She had blond designer-styled hair and wore highly decorative jewelry.

"Hi, I would like to see the director."

The receptionist smiled. "I am the director. My name is Muriel. How can I help you?"

Impressed with her direct, confident air, I looked at her more closely. She did not seem to be the kind of dreamy mystic that I feared might be a money-stealing phony with no real power.

"I am interested in having an in-depth psychic counseling session with you. Can that be arranged?" I asked cautiously.

"Yes," she replied. "Would you like to make an appointment for this coming week?"

Hesitating before replying, I started to become suspicious and wondered what kind of institution this place really was. It had a religious atmosphere that made me uneasy. I was looking for psychic power, not a religious cult. "Are you some kind of religion?"

"No, we are not a religion," Muriel replied. "We are spiritual."

I wasn't sure I understood the difference. However, somehow her assurance prompted me to set up an evening appointment for later that week.

Counseling Session With a New Age Psychic

Feeling a sense of anticipation, I arrived at the

Lighted Way for my appointment. Although still concerned that a psychic might not have any real power, I did not believe this woman to be an outright fraud.

While waiting for Muriel, I noticed a frame on the wall displaying a master's degree diploma from Pepperdine University. Another frame displayed a California license for individual, family, and marriage counseling.

Muriel greeted me and escorted me to a small table. We sat down at opposite sides, facing one another. "What do you need help with?" she asked.

I expressed my need for direction in my life, telling her that I didn't know where I was going or what I should be doing in order to find fulfillment.

Muriel listened to me intently. She then took out a pack of cards and placed them on the table. I recognized them to be tarot cards.

"Muriel," I interrupted. "I really wanted this to be a reading using psychic power coming from the cosmic realms. I'm sorry, but I don't have any respect for fortune-telling cards."

"Oh, I use the cards only to open up the ethers and reveal the Akashic Records," Muriel replied.

Not understanding what she meant, I looked at her with a questioning frown.

"These are the records permanently kept in the heavenlies," she explained. "They describe every event that has occurred, and contain all knowledge. They are like a gigantic, cosmic computer memory. The cards simply start the process of opening me up so that I can psychically read the records and channel the masters."

The "masters"? I wonder who they are, I thought to myself.

"I do not actually need the cards," Muriel assured me. "We will not use them if you feel uncomfortable about them."

"I prefer that we don't use them," I replied.

The interview proceeded. It covered several areas of my life. Periodically Muriel closed her eyes and appeared to be concentrating intently as if listening to some kind of inner voice telling her information. Sometimes she described people and scenes to me, and I had the sense that she was picturing these in her mind as she described them in detail.

During the reading, Muriel clearly described several interesting and intricate aspects of my parents' characters. Her accuracy of revelation was astounding. I had not told Muriel anything about my parents, yet she was able to talk about them as if she were personally acquainted with them.

I started to notice drops of perspiration falling from my forehead. I had to keep wiping my face with a tissue. I thought to myself, This is strange. I feel cool. The room is well air-conditioned. Why am I sweating so much? Throughout the interview large drops of liquid literally rolled down my face. I had never experienced anything like it before.

Holding my fascination, Muriel continued to describe the characters and inner motives of several of my friends. I was amazed at her depth of perception and clear understanding of events. She seemed to be able to churn out information endlessly, like a talking psychic encyclopedia.

I then asked Muriel questions about my job. She had insight about my employment skills and about relationships with colleagues at work.

I asked questions about several personal problems that were bothering me, such as, why had my relationship with my parents been so stormy?

"I am seeing a past life in which you were the father of a little girl," Muriel described. "This girl is now your mother in your present life."

I leaned forward in interest. Muriel had her eyes closed as if focusing upon the cosmic realms. "In this past life you were living as an American Indian. I can clearly see you as a medicine man. You are hugging your beautiful daughter. A lot of conflicts, karma, remained unresolved in this past life. That is why you chose your present mother."

Mmmmm, I thought, did I really choose my mother before I was born?

"I see the relationship improving," Muriel continued. "You will write letters to your mother and clear up a lot of misunderstandings."

There was a moment of silence.

"Your soul's destiny plan for this life is soon going to start working out," Muriel said.

Wow, I thought, this ties in exactly with the strange inner voice that had recently spoken to me concerning my soul. I began to wonder if my interview with Muriel was some kind of event that had been prearranged in the cosmic realms.

Muriel talked more about my destiny as I continued to wipe drops of perspiration from my forehead.

The psychic reading lasted for about an hour and a half. At the end of it, Muriel handed me an attractive brochure and invited me to come to some of the evening classes she gave. I left with a sense of excitement and interest at this new vista of promise before me.

The counseling session was recorded on cassette tapes, which I played several times. The reading had two fascinating aspects. First, I was convinced without doubt that Muriel had definite psychic powers. No ordinary person could have so accurately described the characters of my parents and other associates without having been intimately acquainted with them.

Second, it was amazing how throughout the interview I sweated profusely in spite of feeling comfortably cool and being neither nervous nor excited. So I concluded that some kind of strong, cosmic energy was present during our interaction and had caused my forehead to drip in constant perspiration.

I was intrigued by Muriel's psychic ability to "read" the Akashic Records in order to reveal to me details of my past lives. The concept of reincarnation and past lives had always interested me. The idea seemed to provide answers to a lot of my questions regarding the nature of life: Why should one person be born into miserable sickness and suffering, and another be born into health and a loving, supportive home environment? Is it merely luck at birth? Or is there a just reason for apparent injustices? Perhaps fortunes reverse in other lifetimes so as to achieve a just balance for every soul when averaged over many lifetimes. The idea of reincarnation sounded logical.

This initial psychic reading set the stage for my plunge into the world of mysticism, Eastern religions, and the occult. I was intrigued that Muriel had claimed healing powers and had stated that she was in possession of a whole body of esoteric knowledge, which, if learned, would result in a transformed life and in achieving one's personal, ideal "destiny plan."

My mind was full of questions and ideas concerning my past lives. Could Muriel really tell me more about those deeply hidden inner realms of my soul? Could the unlocking of past-life conflicts possibly help me resolve my problems in this life? Maybe a lot of my irrational fears and anxieties could be traced to unresolved past-life conflicts and trauma. If I could unravel the blockages from those lives, just think of the healing and growth that could take place in me and how my functioning would be enhanced. I could benefit tremendously.

I thought about the possibility of developing increased intuitive abilities. Just think of the possibilities if one were to consistently make correct business decisions when possessing precise intuitive power.

The lure had been tasted. Wanting to gain more of this knowledge and to further experience Muriel's psychic ability, I decided to attend the metaphysical classes. I had been seduced by the display of psychic power.

Chapter 3

Learning the Art of Channeling

The brochure for the Lighted Way metaphysical center listed classes with interesting-sounding names:
astrology, Egyptian tarot, numerology, and psychosynthesis. I was familiar with astrology, but not with the
other subjects.

Muriel, the center's director, had recommended that I
start with the Wednesday evening psychosynthesis class.
From its name, the psychosynthesis class sounded like it
was going to be a program of psychological development.
I hoped this would not be the case. Having had plenty of
psychology, I wanted to learn about esoteric philosophy
and wanted to experience more of the psychic power
Muriel seemed to possess.

I decided to follow her suggestion and attend this
class. I was also eager to ask Muriel who the "masters"
were, those spirit guides with whom she claimed to
communicate.

Wednesday evening finally arrived. I fought my way
through the last of the Los Angeles rush-hour traffic and
arrived at the Lighted Way a little late. The class had already started. A group of ten or twelve people sat in a
circle in the room where the psychic fair had been held.

As I slipped into a vacant seat and scanned the circle
of people around me, I noticed that the members of the
class ranged in age from about twenty-five to fifty. Some

36

of the people looked as if they were young professionals; others may have been secretaries, blue-collar workers, and housewives.

Muriel, wearing jeans and a brightly colored blouse, was talking. "The New Age is going to be a golden age of love, light, and joy," she said. "This new age of Aquarius has actually already started. Powerful new spiritual energies are now radiating upon the planet. Mankind will evolve their consciousness much more quickly as these cosmic energies play upon each individual person."

I wanted to ask Muriel for clarification about these energies, but I was afraid to interrupt. Everyone in the circle had their eyes glued on her like an audience gazing at a singer on center stage.

She continued her talk. "The consciousness of the ordinary person is known as the personality, or lower self. It is concerned with survival and seeking pleasure. It worries about getting money in order to live. It concerns itself with finding friends in order to thwart loneliness and feel secure in a social setting. It aspires to fulfill the instinct to be with a mate and have a family. It involves itself with scholastic and intellectual attainments in order to understand our civilization and function more successfully in the world."

I wanted to get back to these cosmic energies.

"Muriel," I interrupted, raising my hand. "You mentioned cosmic energies. Could you say a little more about where they come from? Are you talking about X-rays, that sort of thing?"

"No, Will," she replied, "these energies are of a much higher vibration than what are found in the world of science. The cosmic energies come from outer space and originate in various star groups, mainly the constellations of astrology. They are divine energies that ultimately come from God. The constellations channel, or direct, these energies to planet Earth. The energies are subtle, but very powerful. They stimulate a person's spiritual nature and affect his physiological system through the chakras."

"Muriel, what are chakras?" someone else in the class asked.

Muriel looked a little impatient. I was relieved to discover I was not the only ignorant one in the class.

"Chakras are the body's own energy 'nerve' centers," she explained. "Five of the centers are located on the spinal column, starting with the base chakra at the bottom. Four other chakra centers are positioned at specific locations up the spine. The sixth chakra is an important one. It is called the 'third-eye center' and is located in your forehead."

Muriel touched the front of her forehead with her hand to show its location. "The seventh center is at the top of your head. It is called the crown chakra."

I wanted to know how the cosmic energies affect these chakras. Luckily, Muriel started to explain it before I had the chance to ask the question. "The New Age aspirant can absorb the cosmic energies during meditation. They will facilitate the development of his consciousness. As the energies are absorbed by the chakras, subtle changes occur in the person's physiology and brain cells. The chakras become more powerful, and the person develops greater awareness and strength of character. New skills and qualities develop that would not be evident if the person was functioning only at his personality level."

Interesting, I thought. So this is why Eastern gurus do so much meditation. Maybe they really do absorb transformative cosmic energy, which makes them wise. Hmmmm, perhaps I will give meditation a try.

Muriel then talked about the necessity of surrendering one's life to God and of seeking to transcend the personality. Its goals needed to be replaced with the desire to seek God, and the will of the personality needed to be given over to the will of God.

"God speaks to us through our higher self," she continued. "Unless we develop our higher self and become sensitive to it, we cannot contact God and become at one with his divine consciousness. The higher self is always inside of us, but in most people, it lies dormant in the subconscious mind. To contact this consciousness, which is wiser than normal intellect, you need to build a bridge from your lower self to your higher self. You will build this bridge to God, symbolized by the rainbow, by coming to these classes and practicing your daily meditation."

I had been thinking about the voice of God speaking to people and wondered what it sounded like. Finally I asked Muriel about it.

"Don't search for a voice that you can hear audibly with your ears," she explained. "It isn't like that. The higher self speaks through your mind as you attune to it. Now at other times, God can speak to us through his emissaries, the masters. But again, the masters will use the vehicle of your higher self in order to communicate with you. They speak through your conscience. With practice, you will be able to identify what comes from the higher realms."

I wondered who these masters were that Muriel kept mentioning.

"The masters may tell us to do things that we ourselves do not want to do," she continued. "The old self, the ego, the personality, rebels. It resists the will of God. You then have to trust that God knows best what should be done. The little will of the personality has to bend to the greater will of God if you are to progress on the path of consciousness development. Only in obedience can you attain Christ-consciousness, that happy union with God."

Muriel described how the masters often instructed her to do things that required a lot of faith and trust. I sensed that the masters were some kind of spirit guides who could communicate with Muriel. She illustrated her point with a practical example.

"Master Koot Hoomi told me to build this attic room and spiral stairway," Muriel said, as she pointed to the stairway at the side of the room. I looked up and noticed that someone had built a beautiful and ornate stairway leading up to a balcony.

"I was not informed why I should build this room," she continued. "I knew it was going to cost a lot of money to have it custom-built just as the master wanted it. I decided to go ahead in faith and do just as I was told, knowing that God had a specific reason for me to carry out this project."

I glanced up at the stairway again, then looked back at Muriel.

"God has always blessed me. Many times I didn't know why he wanted me to do certain things, but I went ahead in faith and did them anyway. I later found out that God knew what he was doing, and it all worked out just wonderfully in the end. You have to learn to trust the voice of God as it is revealed to you in your meditation."

Muriel paused as if pondering what to say next. Should I ask her another question? I thought. I may as well try to learn something while I am here, I concluded.

"Muriel, why are we in a new age?"

"If you look up at the sky at night, you can see the astrological constellations in the heavens, such as Taurus the bull or Aries the ram. If you were to observe these constellations over a year's time, you would find that their positions moved a tiny amount in relation to the background of the universe behind them. Over a period of 2,000 years, the constellations will have moved in the sky by an amount equal to the arc of one of the twelve constellations, like a clock hand moving from three o'clock to four o'clock, say."

I had always wanted to understand astrology. Perhaps I will take a class in it, I thought to myself as Muriel was explaining.

"Over the last 2,000 years, we have been in the sign

of Pisces, and the age has been called the Piscean Age. Recently, we have just moved into the sign of Aquarius, and that is why we are in a new age, called the age of Aquarius. Each age brings in new cosmic energies that produce a change of consciousness on the planet.

"It is time to do our meditation," Muriel announced abruptly.

She walked over to the altar table at the front of the room and lighted two candles and some incense. I noticed that standing at the back of the altar were several framed photographs of people, a couple of whom wore turbans. I wondered if those were possibly pictures of the masters.

The lights in the room were turned very low. Muriel returned to her seat. Everyone in the group closed their eyes and held their hands in their laps. I followed their example.

Muriel spoke. "Sit comfortably with the spine erect. Relax and be at peace in the presence of God."

In the total silence that followed, I started to feel uneasy. I hoped I was not being lured into some sort of cult religion. The dark room and deathly silence gave me the creeps, and I almost sensed a kind of evil atmosphere to the place and thought that maybe this place was not for me in the long term. I consoled myself by reasoning I was just not used to this kind of thing, and the group was probably quite harmless. Concluding that I could always stop coming to the classes if things became too suspicious, I felt more relaxed.

After a few moments of silence, Muriel spoke again.

"Image a ray or beam of golden light coming from the sun. Image it shining upon you. Slowly take in a deep breath. Now visualize the light cascading out of the top of your head like a shower of lights. This ray of light is to open the outer three petals of the heart chakra."[1]

---

1. The heart chakra is claimed by New Agers to be an important energy "nerve" center located near the spine at the level of the heart. In Hinduism it is symbolically pictured as a twelve-petaled lotus flower.

I had difficulty holding the image of the beam of light. My imagination kept wandering away to other things.

Muriel continued to give step-by-step instructions for breathing, for visualizing light, and for reciting short invocations. We finally imagined ourselves seated under a tree in a beautiful garden called the garden of the soul. These techniques were to balance the mind, body, and emotions and to open the person to the higher self and receive communication from the masters.

After about five minutes of silent meditation, Muriel spoke again.

"We invite the presence and the energy of our beloved master, Djwhal Khul."

"Djwhal Khul?" Who is he? I wondered.

"Beloved Djwhal Khul, we are honored with your presence tonight. We admire your qualities of dedication and love. We ask you to come into our group and speak through us and share with us some of your wisdom. We are thankful that we can channel you tonight."

Then Muriel began to speak in a manner somewhat different from her normal speech.

"It pleases me to be here tonight," she said. "There has been an increase in the amount of light in this group over the last few weeks. We in the Hierarchy are very happy at the dedication of the members of this light circle. However, there is still much work to be done."

It seemed that Muriel had been speaking in the first person of the spirit guide Djwhal Khul, as if vocalizing the thoughts that he supposedly wanted to communicate to the group.

I continued to listen with interest but wondered whether Muriel was perhaps just speaking from her own subconscious mind. Maybe this Djwhal Khul was pure imagination creating a more dramatic effect.

"Do not use your minds too much by trying to think out the great mysteries of the divine realms," Muriel channeled. "It is better for you to just meditate in the light and allow the process of divine intuition and illumination to bring you knowledge and wisdom. Too much use of the intellect by a disciple will be a hindrance to his development of higher consciousness. Go directly to the source of all knowledge and wisdom. Listen to the voice of God."

Muriel paused for a moment. I noticed that when she had been channeling Djwhal Khul, her sentence structure was much more refined than her conventional mode of speech. Otherwise, she more or less appeared to be speaking with her regular voice.

She then asked Djwhal Khul for some comments. "Beloved master. Tonight we want to talk about love. We wonder if you have anything to say to us about this beautiful quality."

After a short period of silence, Muriel began to channel Djwhal Khul again.

"Never forget that love is the greatest force in the universe. Love everything around you. Take into your heart the words of my fellow brother, the Master Jesus. When he walked the earth 2,000 years ago, he said that we should love so much that we even love our enemies."

Interesting, I thought. It seems like Djwhal Khul is claiming that Jesus Christ is one of his brothers. I wondered if he was implying that Jesus is one of the masters.

"As the energies of the New Age become more firmly grounded upon the planet," Muriel continued, "you will begin to find that all people at all levels of life will express more brotherly love. This will truly be a golden age of love; it will be the kingdom of heaven manifested on earth, just as the beloved Jesus promised. Do your meditation each day. Live a life of harmlessness and love. I bid you farewell."

A few moments of silence followed.

Muriel then made an announcement. "We are going to go around the light circle in sequence and channel Master Jesus."

I felt uneasy. This thing was getting too much like religion.

"I want you to relax," she instructed. "When it is your turn to channel, just verbalize any thoughts that you have in your mind. Think of it as being a process of channeling the thoughts of your higher self as you sit in meditation. We will begin with Larry and go round the circle clockwise."

I wondered what would happen when it came to my turn. Never having done this kind of thing before, I was afraid that I might become possessed, or, worse still, that perhaps nothing would happen and I wouldn't know what to say. I didn't want to be embarrassed in front of the group. Perhaps you have been in that kind of situation.

Muriel began the group channeling with a short invocation.

"We see Larry surrounded by golden light and aligned to his higher self," she said. "In the energy of our beloved Master Jesus, we ask that Larry bring forth a message of truth for us."

Larry channeled a message in the same manner that Muriel had done previously, but the message was a little shorter.

Muriel went around the group to each member in sequence. She repeated the invocation and then allowed each person to channel a message, purportedly coming from Master Jesus.

As one of the group members was channeling a message, all of a sudden the inside of my forehead lighted up with bright light. It was as if someone had switched on an electric light bulb inside the front of my brain.

At first I thought that perhaps someone had switched on the room light. I opened my eyes and saw only the darkness of the room. I closed my eyes again. The bright light was still there. I was definitely not imagining a light. It seemed as if a tangible physiological change had taken place in my brain cells whereby suddenly the front part of my brain had been lighted up. I felt a pleasant feeling of relaxation and peace and wondered whether this mystical effect was the result of cosmic energy beaming upon my third-eye chakra supposedly located in the forehead.

Soon my turn to channel came. Muriel repeated the invocation. I sat quietly for a few moments and wondered what I was supposed to say. I felt hesitant to speak in case I said the wrong thing. In my mind, all I could think were the words "love one another."

I said, "Love one another."

Muriel immediately passed on to the next person. Eventually all the group had a turn at channeling.

After a few moments of silence, Muriel spoke again. "This week in your meditations at home I want you to go into your soul's garden and sit under a lilac-colored tree of strength. Meditating under it will give you strength and develop your will."

There was another pause.

Muriel continued with instructions on visualizing the light from her center being spread to the entire United States, to the President and government officials in Washington, D.C., to the United Nations organization, and finally spreading around the entire planet Earth.

"Let us say three Om's," announced Muriel.

In unison, the group chanted three long sounds, taking a deep breath each time, "Oooooooommmmmmmmm-mmm."

The noise was quite loud. I wondered whether anyone in the commercial office next door could hear it and what they thought. After the final Om, the entire group followed Muriel's lead and recited a prayer, which was referred to as The Great Invocation. I was not familiar with its words and remained silent.

As I drove home from class, my mind was full of questions. Who are these masters, such as Djwhal Khul, whom we were supposedly channeling? Is Jesus Christ really still alive somewhere? How many masters are there? Are they humans, like living gurus, or are they spirit beings like ghosts, existing without any physical body? In what way were the masters related to God? Was Jesus really one of a group of masters?

The fact that Muriel talked about God and Jesus Christ made me uneasy. I did not want to be drawn into a religious cult. I rationalized that the masters were probably all in Muriel's imagination and, in reality, she was just speaking from the subconscious depths of her own mind. But I couldn't explain the mysterious light that had suddenly shone inside my brain. What was it? I certainly wasn't imagining it. Where did it come from? How would it affect me? Curiosity about the light helped me to decide to attend class the following week.

Wednesday evening finally arrived. The format of the class was very similar to the previous week's session. Amazingly, at one point during the group meditation, the front of my brain again suddenly lighted up as if a light bulb had been switched on inside my head. This time Muriel was invoking the presence and energy of a master called Lord Maitreya. She referred to him as being "the Christ." I had always assumed that Jesus was Christ, but apparently Maitreya had this title also, whatever it was supposed to mean.

When it was my turn to channel, Muriel repeated the invocation: "We see Will in a sphere of golden Christ light. He is aligned to his higher self to bring forth a message of wisdom from Lord Maitreya."

"The energies of the New Age are now much stronger on the planet," I said hesitantly. "The changes taking place in civilization will speed up. This will cause some turmoil and negative side effects, but in the end, the golden age will be ushered in, and mankind will be blessed."

This time I noticed I was able to channel a longer message than I had the previous week. I started out with just a single idea in my mind. I didn't know where the idea came from, but as I began to speak, the words just seemed to flow out of me. Soon, however, the words stopped.

After everyone in the circle had a turn at channeling, Muriel announced, "We are now going to split into groups of three and do triad channeling. Take turns to channel each other psychic messages that come from your higher self."

The people in the light circle split up into groups of three. Muriel introduced me to two women with whom I was to work. One of the women, Rosie, was a pretty and likable woman in her mid-twenties. We sat on the carpeted floor in a triangle formation. It was agreed that Rosie would start first and channel me a personal message. We closed our eyes as if in meditation. The other woman started to speak. "We see Rosie in the center of a triangle of golden light," she said. "In this Christ light[2] Rosie is aligned to her higher self and is able to bring forth a message of wisdom for Will."

I opened my eyes and relaxed as Rosie meditated for a few moments.

When she started to speak, the words came very slowly and with difficulty, as if she were straining in order to psychically perceive a message entering her mind. "You have recently been thinking about a certain woman," said Rosie. "She has had a very strong influence in your life in the past. Her name is Jenny . . . Jenny J . . . Jenny Jame. . . ."

I was absolutely stunned. What Rosie had said was astoundingly accurate. I had known a woman named Jenny James when I lived back in England. Jenny was a psychologist and personal friend who had been a radi-

---

2. In New Age terminology, "Christ light" denotes a cosmic energy, believed to be one of seven fundamental spiritual energies (called "rays") that permeate the universe. It is known as the "second ray" energy and supposedly gives the qualities of love and wisdom when it operates. New Agers believe that Jesus Christ utilized "Christ energy" during his Palestinian mission, but they do not regard Jesus as being the source of the energy.

cal influence in my life.

Rosie continued. "She has long black hair. Your relationship with her was not a romance; it was platonic, but very powerful nonetheless. An intense and special relationship."

I was utterly amazed. Everything Rosie had said was correct. I had not had any contact with Jenny for about three years, but I still regarded her as a special influence in my life. She was a New Ager and had introduced me to astrology.

I eagerly waited for Rosie to speak more.

Finally she said, "You will not have contact with her again."

With excitement I told Rosie and the other woman that everything channeled had been 100 percent accurate.

At the end of the class, I went over to the hospitality area and spoke to Rosie. "Rosie, have you been involved in this kind of channeling activity for a long time?"

"No, not at all," she replied. "In fact this is the first class that I have attended."

I was surprised by her answer. I had automatically assumed that she must have been an experienced channeler. "You mean you have never done channeling before coming to this class tonight?" I asked.

"That's right. This is the first time."

"Wow," I exclaimed. "You have incredible psychic ability."

I hurried over to the bookstore area. I wanted to get some books about this new body of knowledge to which I had been exposed. I wanted to learn more about this power and to know who the masters were, those spirit intelligences who were supposedly intimately involved with the Lighted Way. I made a purchase and left the center with a couple of books tucked under my arm. I was excited about what had happened.

My initial skepticism about the channeling techniques had now been thoroughly demolished. For me, Rosie's channeling was absolute proof that in the state of meditation it was possible to reach into areas of consciousness and knowledge normally inaccessible when using one's regular thinking processes. I was even more impressed with Rosie's channeling than I had been with Muriel's psychic abilities. When I had the psychic reading with Muriel, she had not attempted to speak out the actual name of a person with whom I was acquainted. Further, Rosie had perfectly described my friend Jenny's appearance and character. That was astounding!

If I had been thinking about Jenny James at the time of Rosie's channeling, I could have concluded that Rosie simply had been able to read my mind, a feat commendable in itself. However, I had not been thinking about Jenny that evening. I concluded that whatever the "higher self" was, it had definite access to the cosmic realms of hidden knowledge.

The lighting up of my brain area during the meditation and the channeling with Rosie made me much more willing to accept the knowledge and ideas promoted in the metaphysics books I had purchased. I was determined to study the books thoroughly and become fully familiar with the tenets of this exciting world of New Age metaphysics.

Chapter 4

The Higher Self Takes Control

I didn't know how I was going to tell Cathy the bad news. A feeling of uneasiness and embarrassment filled me as I sat beside her. Her curly brown hair rested gently on her shoulders, and she looked cute in her blue jeans and pink sweater. Cathy and I had been dating for several weeks. We had planned to spend the afternoon together down at the beach.

How on earth was I going to explain things to her? The news had been a big surprise to me. I never expected it. It came to me as soon as I had awakened that morning. It was like my higher self manifested as an inner voice of conscience that spoke to me in a very clear manner.

Something deep inside me knew that the higher self was not kidding. I could tell. Upon hearing the instruction, I had been affected on a deep level, as if a tension had been set up inside me.

I struggled to think of the right words. I wanted to tell her the news later that day, sort of break it to her gently. But the voice had said, "No. She must be told as soon as you meet her."

The tension inside was driving me nuts.

"Errrr, Cathy."

Swallowing hard on the lump in my throat, I tried again. "Cathy, listen."

"What?" she replied in an uninterested manner, her eyes looking at something in the room.

"I have some bad news for you."

She did not move.

"It's over. We have to stop seeing one another."

I was surprised how easily the words finally came out. Cathy didn't respond. I wondered whether she had understood.

"What!" she cried suddenly as she jerked her head toward me. "What do you mean?"

"It's over between us. You have to go. I don't know how to explain it."

By now Cathy was looking at me intently.

"It has nothing to do with you," I quickly reassured her. "It is something inside me. It is hard for me to describe, but I woke up this morning and just knew we had to split up."

Cathy looked shocked. She said, "You didn't say anything about this yesterday evening. I thought we were having a wonderful time."

I went blank and remained silent as if I had been struck dumb.

"Will, are you sure you are all right?" she asked with a look of concern.

"Cathy, I'm fine. Believe me, this has nothing to do with you. You have not done anything wrong. I just feel I need some space to, to, er, to study my spiritual books."

I started to feel nervous, really uncomfortable. I told her that I needed to get a drink of water and then left the room just to break the tension. Pacing around the kitchen, I recalled what had happened that morning as soon as I woke up. The inner voice of conscience had clearly spoken to me.

"End your relationship with Cathy," it had said. "She has got to go. You need more time to study the metaphysical books."

Having enjoyed Cathy as a regular date, I didn't want

to sever our relationship. But I could see she was a hindrance to my serious study of the metaphysical books.

I consoled myself with the thought that perhaps the masters intended for me to marry a soul mate at some point in the future when the time was right. As for Cathy, she hadn't known what to think about my interest in metaphysics. Now she was going to conclude that I was completely crazy.

Returning to the living room, I noticed that tears were running down her cheeks. I started to feel awful.

I stood motionless for a few moments, not knowing what to do. Then I sat down beside her and put my arm around her.

"Cathy, I am sorry. I am really sorry for this. Believe me, I am not upset with you or anything like that."

"Then why don't you want our relationship to continue?" she asked in a choking voice.

"It is all a matter of destiny," I replied.

She did not move or say anything, but sat there quietly staring into space. I felt embarrassed. And yet I felt resolute about what I was doing and had no second thoughts about it. The decision was final. I intuitively knew that it had to be this way.

Getting up, I asked Cathy whether she would like some coffee. She shook her head. Tears still rolled down her cheeks. A few minutes of silence passed. I finally walked toward the front door. Cathy followed.

Turning around, I gave her a big hug. We parted and went our separate ways.

It had been a couple of months since I had started attending classes at the Lighted Way. I was now eager to start serious study of the metaphysical books I had purchased.

One of the classes held at the Lighted Way was a systematic study of the book *Treatise on White Magic*, written by Alice Bailey. I found the book fascinating. It claimed that the spirit guide Djwhal Khul had telepathically dictated the contents of *White Magic* to Alice Bailey, a disciple of the masters. She lived in America and acted as a scribe for the penning of the book manuscript, beginning her work in 1919. The Lighted Way carried approximately twenty different titles dictated by Djwhal Khul to Alice Bailey. I had purchased several and now began to study them in detail.

As I studied these metaphysical books and attended the classes at the Lighted Way, I began to realize that my connection with the Lighted Way was by no means accidental. I regarded my association with this metaphysical center to be part of my destiny plan for this lifetime. I believed that "divine" intent had led me to Muriel in order to receive training from her and evolve my consciousness. I regarded it as my destiny to be part of the New Age movement, that great manifestation of "God's" plan for planet Earth.

A few weeks after the split with Cathy, the engine in my green Ford Pinto blew up. Dense blue smoke belched out of its smelly exhaust. Having worked at one time as a car mechanic, I diagnosed that a piston had disintegrated and decided to strip the engine and replace the broken part.

I had always performed my own car repairs, no matter how major the job. I once owned a new car, but found it a bore because it never needed working on. I tended to own older cars because I knew I could take care of any necessary repairs and service. It was part of my way of life.

Shortly after the engine blowup, I got up early one Saturday morning to carry out the repair. Everything was prepared. I had rented an engine hoist and had cleared a space in the garage so that I could work efficiently.

I ate breakfast rather quickly, because I was anxious to get on with the major surgery to the engine. I normally did a meditation right after breakfast, but on this particular morning, I decided to skip it.

As I was putting on my mechanic's coveralls, I heard the inner voice of conscience prompting me to do the meditation. But being in a hurry to start on the car, I ignored the voice. However, it persisted until I finally heeded the advice and decided to meditate for only five minutes or so.

Sitting down cross-legged on the carpet in my bedroom, I tried to get as comfortable as possible. Wearing coveralls did not help. After going through the invocation and visualization ritual taught at the Lighted Way, I sat in the silence of meditation.

My inner thinking became amazingly clear. The inner voice of conscience spoke. "You are completely wasting your time repairing the old Pinto," it said. "You are indulging in an old habit pattern that is now obsolete. Scrap the car and buy yourself a brand new vehicle."

My higher self then explained that instead of spending precious time in the maintenance of old cars, I should be devoting most of my spare time to meditation, contemplation, and the study of New Age literature. "You need to gain a much deeper understanding of the knowledge expounded in the Alice Bailey metaphysical books," the inner voice advised.

I was amazed how clear and logical my thinking became as I did the meditation. It was as if a whole new way of perceiving things had opened up. I could clearly see the folly of my old thinking and behavioral pattern. Even though my "personality" liked the challenge of rebuilding engines, I could see that I was wasting valuable time and energy.

My personality thinking now protested that I did not have the financial resources to buy a new car. It reasoned that I should repair the Pinto as planned, but then sell it so as to have more money for the down payment on a new car.

"You are still thinking in old ways," the higher self interjected. "Let go of the old self. Poverty consciousness is an obsolete attitude. It will hinder your development and growth. You should scrap the car and trust God that all your financial needs will be taken care of."

Reluctantly deciding to step forward in faith, I ended the meditation with a recitation of The Great Invocation. Standing up, I took off the coveralls and phoned the wreckers to make arrangements for scrapping the old car.

The process of meditation seemed to have worked in a very practical way. It was amazing how clearly my higher self had told me it was foolish to keep repairing the old Pinto. Listening to the inner voice enabled me to break the old pattern of thought and action. I could now understand what Muriel was talking about when she claimed that a process of transformation would occur as one responded to the wisdom of the higher self.

I could see that if my old personality were left to operate as it had done for years, there was no way I could change and expand my consciousness into new and wiser methods of dealing with situations. Muriel constantly stressed the need for the higher self to take control and dominate the personality. The lower self, with its old habit patterns and inefficient methods of functioning, had to be released. She emphasized that the only avenue to the superior consciousness of the higher self was through the practice of meditation.

The counsel regarding experience with the Ford Pinto made me strongly aware of how much I needed to change. I became excited about the possibilities that lay ahead if I were to continue practicing meditation. Perhaps I could become very wise and develop acute business acumen. Maybe I would develop talents that I was not even aware I possessed. If I could tap into cosmic power and wisdom, I thought, a whole new vista of exciting vocational possibilities could open up before me. Perhaps I could become a political leader, helping to carry out the will of the masters in the arena of government.

Later that week, I received clear directions during meditation to purchase a specific model of car. The voice of conscience specified, "Get a Plymouth Champ. It is the car for you. The masters want you to have a Champ."

I could not understand why I should purchase this particular model. It would not have been my choice of new car. I rebelled against the direction and set off to visit the local Volkswagen dealer to inspect a Scirocco, a model that had attracted my attention.

As I drove to the dealer in a borrowed pickup, the inner voice of conscience started to speak to me. It was as clear as if I had been in meditation. It said, "Get a Plymouth Champ; you are wasting your time visiting the Volkswagen dealer. Buy a Plymouth Champ; it is the best car for you."

I was surprised to hear my conscience speaking in this distinct manner. I actually resented its intrusion into my plans for the day. I wanted to be free to choose my own car. What surprised me the most was that I could perceive the voice even though I was driving down a highway. I began to wonder if it really was the voice of my higher self; perhaps it was just rubbish in my mind, subconscious nonsense.

Ignoring the pleas of my conscience, I continued on to the Volkswagen dealer. The Scirocco felt wonderful as I test drove it around the streets. Suddenly the voice of conscience interjected, "You are wasting your time. The masters want you to buy a Plymouth Champ." It protested, "It is the best car for you. Obey your higher self. We know what is best for you. Forget the Volkswagen and buy a Plymouth Champ."

The Volkswagen salesman tried his best to sell me on the Scirocco, but he did not realize he was competing against an unseen advisor.

I drove away from the dealer irritated by the fact that my voice of conscience had pestered me again. I had planned to visit the Toyota dealer next, so I headed there.

About halfway there, the voice spoke out again: "Why don't you listen? We have told you already that the Champ is the best car for you. You are wasting your time going to the Toyota dealer. Buy a Plymouth Champ."

I wondered, Who is the "we" that the voice talked about? Could it be that the masters were talking to me through the medium of my higher self?

The voice was so distinct that I pulled off the highway and parked the pickup. I decided to meditate right there in the vehicle. After going through the usual invocation and imagery ritual, I relaxed into meditation. The same inner voice of conscience began to speak again.

"Get the Plymouth Champ," it gently advised. "It is the right car for you. You will like it."

I thought about how wise the advice had been to junk my Pinto. I could also see that my income was more than sufficient to buy a new car, even though my personality had initially protested that I did not have enough money. The higher self surely knew what it was doing.

I decided to try an experiment. I agreed to do exactly what the inner voice was telling me. If it turned out that the Champ was a bad car, then I would know that this inner voice of conscience was an unreliable source of technical guidance.

I turned around and headed for the Plymouth dealer. "You are doing the right thing. Don't bother to look at any other cars. Get the Champ," the voice confirmed as I drove away.

I was surprised how persistent the inner voice had been. It seemed to be able to burst into my thinking at any time. Yet the voice definitely didn't think as I normally thought. I concluded that it must be my higher self and that it could operate outside of meditation almost as clearly as during meditation. It seemed that the masters, or possibly the spirit of "God," was able to speak to me directly through this voice of conscience.

I eventually made a deal on a Champ. It was a wonderful car, and I enjoyed it immensely.

I came to believe that if I aligned my life to the voice of the higher self, "God" would bless me. I strove to develop a faith that would allow me to hand my life over to the will of "God" expressed to me through the higher self. I believed that by so doing, I would come into the abundance and joy of the New Age and would experience both a material blessing and an abundance of happiness as I fulfilled my destiny plan.

After practicing meditation for a few months, I was able to more clearly perceive the still, silent voice of my inner mind. It also became much easier for me to verbalize this inner voice during the group channeling sessions. The secret seemed to lie in the ability to differentiate the voice of the higher self from the voice of the regular intelligence, the personality—an ability developed by practice and perseverance.

The channeling I did in the groups started out as a verbalization of the thoughts from my higher self. As I began to speak, the words would then come out under their own volition, and I could channel long messages. When we channeled the masters, it was my understanding that the master was speaking through the higher self of the person doing the channeling. I desired to be used by the masters as a medium for carrying out their divine work.

I noticed that the strange golden-white light in the front of my forehead was now often present during my meditations. Sometimes the light was lilac or violet colored.

I finally asked Muriel about the light.

She told me that it was caused by an energization of the third-eye center, a major chakra located near the pineal gland in the front part of the brain. She emphasized that meditation causes physiological changes in the brain cells as the light does its transformative work.

From my study of the metaphysical books, I learned that the third-eye center is supposedly an energy center, or chakra, linked to the development of intuition and psychic power. It is postulated that the act of meditation facilitates the absorption of cosmic energy into the various chakras in order to raise their energy levels and promote the development of divine powers.

Muriel explained that the development of the third-eye center would give a person etheric vision, an ability to see into the spirit realms—to have spirit vision, so to speak. Supposedly when this center is fully developed, one can psychically perceive distant places and events, and even see the presence of angels or other spirit beings. I looked forward to developing these abilities.

It appeared that the main goal of the training at the Lighted Way was to enable a person to attune to his higher self and use it as a source of guidance and wisdom. Over and over Muriel stressed that one can reach his higher self only through meditation. She also emphasized that a bridge needed to be built between the lower self (the personality) and the higher self (the soul or God self).

In metaphysical terminology, this bridge, called the "antahkarana," is symbolized by a rainbow and is commonly referred to as the "rainbow bridge." This explains why the rainbow is a common New Age symbol. Of course it does not have the same meaning as its Christian counterpart, which symbolizes God's covenant with Noah.

I was taught that one must experience a transformation in lifestyle and consciousness as one strove to discipline himself and bring his personality under the control of the soul.

For example, if I had outrightly refused to obey the voice of my higher self when it told me to break the relationship with Cathy, the development of my consciousness would have been severely curtailed, no matter how much meditating I did. The classes constantly stressed that obedience to the higher self is a very important requirement for progress to be made on the path of God-consciousness.

The parting with Cathy, the scrapping of the Pinto, and the purchase of the Champ were all moves of obedience on my part that were the first steps in a process of allowing the voice of the higher self to completely take over my life. I gradually began to receive all kinds of "directions"—usually during meditation—that resulted in drastic changes in my life.

Chapter 5

The Master Appears

Imagine you are in a secluded place. Suddenly in front of you appears a shining person radiating intense golden-white light that almost blinds you by its brilliance. He also emanates a soothing presence, filling you with a beautiful sense of peace as you stare transfixed by his radiance.

In an amazing appearance, a dazzling person like this stood before me on the morning of October 30, 1981, about a year after I had started attending classes at the Lighted Way. When I first saw him, my own initial thought was, He looks just like Jesus Christ.

On the morning of the master's appearance, as I pulled myself out of bed, little did I anticipate that I was about to experience an incredible life-changing event. I was about to be taken into the innermost depths of mystical experience and would never again perceive the world in the same way.

After showering, I returned to the bedroom to do my morning meditation. It was a condition of class membership at the Lighted Way that each student should engage in a private meditation session every day. In the Hindu/Buddhist type of meditation that the Lighted Way taught, it was desirable for the meditator to hold his spine as erect as possible, supposedly to enable a free flowing of the energies associated with the chakras.

I usually had difficulty doing my meditation because of a painful back problem that has plagued me since childhood.

This morning was no exception. I felt very uncomfortable as I began to sit cross-legged upon the carpeted floor of my bedroom. The pain in my back prompted me to consider cutting the session short. But I then remembered the words of warning expressed by Master Djwhal Khul in one of his books: "It is impossible to progress along the spiritual path except through the practice of meditation."

I heeded the advice and disciplined myself to sit upright as best as I could. After carrying out the preliminary invocations and prayers, I sat still in meditation. Fighting my back pain, I struggled to keep my torso straight, knowing that the posture needed to be correct for the meditation to be effective. After about three minutes of discomfort and irritability, I had to get up and stretch. I was again tempted to abandon the session and leave the house for my job as an engineer. I just didn't seem to be in the mood for meditation. But the inner voice of conscience prompted me to give it one more try. I again sat down on the floor, crossed my legs, closed my eyes, and repeated the main invocation ritual.

The Mysterious Enveloping Force

I had been meditating for only about four or five minutes. The discomfort in my back was intense, and I had difficulty sitting still. Cramps afflicted my legs as if I had been chained in stocks for several hours.

Suddenly, a physical force that I had never felt before seemed to come upon me. Brilliant light filled my whole being, as if my whole body had become an incandescent lamp. I felt and perceived this sphere of light to be encompassing me and permeating every cell of my body. My brain, especially, was flooded with light, as if a thousand-watt bulb had been switched on inside of my head.

I noticed I had lost all sense of weight and discomfort. The backache was gone. The mysterious force now acted dynamically upon my posture. It felt as if someone very strong took ahold of my torso and forcefully straightened my back and shoulders until I was held fully upright. All remnants of muscular tension had entirely disappeared.

I did not feel any sense of apprehension over what was happening. On the contrary, I felt a deep sense of peace. I noticed I had lost all sense of gravity, as if I were completely weightless and were levitating just above the floor. Yet at the same time I was very much aware that I was still sitting in a corner of my bedroom. My mind, my rational thinking, was still functioning normally, with clear and precise, logical thoughts. I had not taken any kind of drugs whatsoever.

The Master Appears

Suddenly, a man radiating intense golden-white light stood before me. My first perception was that the mysterious, shining figure looked just like Jesus Christ.

Immediately a strong intuitive thought, or "knowingness," surfaced that told me this person was Djwhal Khul, the high-ranking member of the White Brotherhood of Masters. He was the master who had dictated to Alice Bailey the contents of the metaphysical books she had published under her own name.

He appeared to be surrounded by so much brilliance that I could not make out any background scenery. All I could see was his kingly form surrounded by light as he stood motionless before me.

I noticed his curly golden hair resting upon his shoulders. He wore a long white robe. His arms hung at his side, and his feet were hidden by the light that enshrouded his entire being. Even though I had difficulty distinguishing his facial features because of the intensity of light that seemed to emanate more strongly from his face, he looked very handsome and dignified.

In spite of the fact that I was enveloped in intense cosmic energy, my mind and intelligence did not in any way feel hypnotized or "possessed" by Djwhal Khul's presence. I had sharp clarity and awareness in my thinking.

"How are you doing?" Djwhal Khul asked me.

I noticed his lips did not move when he spoke. The communication seemed to be transmitted telepathically. I perceived his message clearly, but seemed to hear it with an "inner ear," as if his voice were speaking directly into the inside of my mind.

After asking the question, he waited for my reply.

"Well, I am struggling on in my spiritual life," I calmly told him.

I spoke to him with my mind rather than by using lips and vocal chords. It was as if I telepathically communicated my statement. I somehow "knew" that Djwhal Khul could understand me and was able to respond through direct return communication.

Djwhal Khul then commented nonchalantly, "Yes. Well, that is how it is." I sensed the gesture of shrugging his shoulders.

Feeling relaxed and at ease, I then took the initiative to ask him about a specific health problem that had been bothering me for some time. I was eager for his reply.

"Don't worry about it," he simply commented.

After a few moments of silence on his part, he suddenly disappeared, leaving behind the intense aura of brilliant light, which slowly began to dissipate. Simultaneously, physical sensation began to return. My back posture started to sag, and I became aware that I was sitting in an uncomfortable cross-legged posture.

The light and the mysterious force that had filled my whole being now vanished. I moved my aching muscles and became conscious of the fact that I had suddenly resumed breathing. Apparently it had been unnecessary to breathe while in the presence of the great master.

I got up to stretch my legs and then sat on the bed to think about the meaning of this experience.

Wow! I thought, I have made it to something big.

I recalled Djwhal Khul's teachings, as recorded in Alice Bailey's books, of how a dedicated aspirant on the metaphysical path can eventually receive a reward for his efforts. He can receive the honor of being made a personal disciple of one of the masters of the White Brotherhood. The master then appears to the disciple to confirm the master-disciple relationship.

Regarding myself as one of the luckiest people in Los Angeles that morning, I was delighted to have been selected for training as a personal disciple of one of the masters. I was especially excited by the fact that I had been accepted as a disciple by the distinguished Master Djwhal Khul, the master whose books I had so reverently appreciated and loved to study. Oh, how much I admired the wisdom contained in his writings. I had never read anything so captivating and intellectually inspiring. For me, his works had relegated the knowledge of Kant, Aristotle, and Sartre to the kindergarten level.

I felt privileged that I could now serve "God" by serving under his noble agent, my master, the venerable Djwhal Khul. It was as if my highest dream and ambition had come true.

I recalled how only a few days previously I had taken a private vow of celibacy. It appeared that "God" had truly rewarded me for my decision to renounce women and sex and to seek the things of "God" by making me a disciple to one of the masters. I knew I would face much hardship on the discipleship path, but I had faith that the forces of the heavenly realms would assist me.

I was thankful to "God" that I had been through the emotional hardships and feelings of dissatisfaction that had prompted me to search for existential knowledge; for they had led me to seek wisdom, understanding, harmony, and fulfillment of my life's destiny plan. Now at last, the master's appearance seemed to give me tangible proof that I had been searching in the right direction.

Suddenly realizing that I would be late for work if I sat around any longer, I headed out of the house and jumped into my car. During the twenty-six-mile drive to work, I thought of nothing except the privilege of being a disciple of Djwhal Khul. I wondered where my life would now lead, but I really didn't care. All that mattered was that I must serve the master.

After arriving at work, I started to feel tired. Normally I am a fairly energetic worker, but on this morning I had difficulty concentrating on my job. As the morning progressed, I felt more and more fatigued. By about eleven, I felt absolutely exhausted, both mentally and physically. I could hardly stand up, and every muscle in my body ached as if I had just completed a twenty-six mile marathon. I had never felt so exhausted in my life, not even during a severe bout of influenza. I told my supervisor that I was feeling very sick, and I returned home, where I collapsed in total exhaustion and slept for hours.

The visitation of Djwhal Khul involved a colossal depletion of my energy reserves. I recalled the apostle Paul's blindness and weakness after his initial encounter with Christ on the road to Damascus. Reasoning that one doesn't get exhausted from dreams, vivid imagination, or hallucinations lasting for only three or four minutes, I knew that whatever happened to me was real and involved a massive taxing of my energy system. I had not been involved in any kind of drug taking.

Any lingering doubts in my mind regarding the existence of spirit beings were now demolished forever. The dramatic visitation by Djwhal Khul relegated the philosophies of materialistic atheism to the level of absurdity. I now had total faith in the New Age movement and its array of metaphysical teachings.

Spirit Guides and Their Master-work of Deception

Djwhal Khul's books fascinated me. I had read several

of his volumes with great enthusiasm and had become captivated by his apparently vast knowledge regarding the realms of God and the way God interacted with humanity through the medium of spiritual energies, spirit beings, and masters such as Djwhal Khul himself and Master Jesus. Djwhal Khul's books had the power to radically transform my life: to completely change the way I thought, the way I viewed the world, and the way I perceived my destiny.

By means of telepathic communication, Djwhal Khul was able to dictate verbatim the contents of twenty-five volumes of esoteric metaphysical knowledge through a woman named Alice Bailey. The books, published between the years of 1919 and 1949, provide much of the doctrinal basis for what has now emerged as the New Age movement. Amazingly, at one time Alice Bailey was a devout Christian and wife of an Episcopal priest before she became influenced by friends who belonged to the Theosophical Society.

In his Alice Bailey–authored books, Djwhal Khul claims that he is a senior member of a group of people called the Hierarchy of Masters. He has deceived many people into thinking he is an emissary from God. In reality, he is one of the main spirit beings orchestrating the New Age movement.

He maintains that he is a human being born more than 350 years ago in Tibet, where he was at one time the abbot of a Tibetan lamasery. He asserts that through the process of meditation and strict spiritual practices, and through the assistance of heavenly beings, he has so evolved his consciousness as to have reached a state of immortality in his current physical body. Hence his claimed ability to have lived for almost four centuries.

Djwhal Khul claims that his immortality was bestowed by means of an initiation ceremony held in the heavenly realms, called the "fifth initiation" (also known as the "ascension," "Christhood," or "mastership" initiation). As a result of this cosmic initiation, Djwhal Khul alleges that he became a member of an elite group of human beings who describe themselves as being "ascended masters" and who have attained immortality, never to again be reincarnated.

"Jesus Christ" and the Hierarchy of Masters

In his metaphysical works, Djwhal Khul contends that forty-nine human beings presently living on the planet—most of them in remote areas of the Himalayas—are ascended masters. As a group organization, he calls them the "Hierarchy of Masters" (also "the White Brotherhood," "the Masters of Wisdom," "the Hierarchy," or simply, "the Masters"). The leader of the Hierarchy, a master called Lord Maitreya, holds the executive office, or title of "the Christ."

Djwhal Khul claims that "Jesus Christ" is a senior-ranking member of the Hierarchy of Masters and asserts that the great legendary gurus of India, such as the Buddha, also form part of the brotherhood. He contends that the Hierarchy are working for the spiritual evolution of humanity on planet Earth in all its aspects: religious, political, technological, scientific, and cultural.

Djwhal Khul specifically teaches that Master Jesus is alive on the planet, busily directing the destiny of Christianity by telepathically transmitting ideas into the subconscious minds of the leaders of the Christian church. He emphasizes that Master Jesus is a man who evolved himself over successive incarnations and initiations until he became an immortal "Son of God," just as the other masters, such as the Buddha, also became "Sons of God."

According to Djwhal Khul, the masters can exit their physical bodies and travel around in their "soul" or "spirit" bodies to any location on the planet, unimpeded by distance or time. A master also supposedly has the power to condense his spirit body into a visible body of light, called the *anuvarrupa* in Hindu terminology. Thus the master would be in his *anuvarrupa* body when he appeared to someone as a shining being of dazzling light, just as Djwhal Khul appeared to me. The master can, at will, condense his spirit body into a physical form and be seen, touched, and experienced as a regular human being.

The New World Religion

Djwhal Khul claims that as part of his work for "God," he was assigned the special project of bringing to humanity the New Age teachings for the New World Religion. Designed to integrate Christianity and the Eastern teachings of Hinduism and Buddhism into a homogeneous wholeness, the New World Religion pretends to reveal the full expression of divinity in all its aspects. Djwhal Khul asserts he received most of his knowledge directly from his own superiors in heaven.

His books have found their way across the globe. They cover a wide range of topics—from cause of illness, psychoses, and demonic possession to development of intellect, growth of civilizations, and economic cycles. Thousands of people have completely changed their lifestyles as a result of his writings. I myself became so overwhelmed by Djwhal Khul's concepts and his intellectual genius that I revered him as a great saint.

Perhaps the most important—and the most deceptive—are Djwhal Khul's teachings about the Holy Bible. He demonstrates a vast knowledge concerning the major religions of the world and even comments about the nature of God Almighty, the Most High, and the operations of the heavenly throne.

One statement especially caught my attention:

> What do we mean by that phrase "forces of evil"? Not the armies of unrighteousness and sinfulness, organized under that figment of the imagination, the devil, or some supreme antichrist. For such an army does not exist, and

there is no great enemy of God, arraigned in battle against the Most High. There is only suffering, erring humanity.

I found his statement a brilliant confirmation of what I had believed for many years: Satan did not exist. Djwhal Khul then went on to describe just what the forces of evil were:

The forces of evil are, in the last analysis, only the entrenched ancient ideals and habits of thought which have served their purpose in bringing the race to its present point of development, but which must now disappear if the New Age is to be ushered in as desired.

Slavery to the Masters

Impressed by his vast knowledge, I felt honored to become Djwhal Khul's obedient and devoted disciple. Eventually, however, the esteemed discipleship turned into a nightmare of slavery.

I had little money, but gradually I was forced to give everything I had to support his New Age cause. Eventually I devoted all of my time to the furtherance of his work. In obeying his teachings and commands, I believed I was serving God. In return, I was promised healing and happiness, abundance and joy. I was even promised immortality in this lifetime. Not one promise was to have lasting fulfillment.

I became one of the many people who are now consciously serving the masters and the other spirit guides through a direct and personal relationship with them. On a global basis, millions of people are being lured into following the inner guidance of their "higher consciousness" through meditation and other consciousness-raising techniques. Opening the door of the mind to the "higher self" really does allow one to contact the realms of "the spirit." At the time, I never suspected that the powers of the spirit world that I was turning to were those same powers that the apostle Paul warned about in his message to the church at Ephesus:

> We are not fighting against people made of flesh and blood, but against persons without bodies—the evil rulers of the unseen world, those mighty satanic beings and great evil princes of darkness who rule this world; and against huge numbers of wicked spirits in the spirit world (Ephesians 6:12, LB).

Djwhal Khul's specialty is counterfeit religion. He is a master forger who tries to lead even the elect astray, if that were possible. As a Christian, you need to be aware of the activities of Djwhal Khul and his colleagues. Masquerading as Jesus Christ, they sometimes appear to Christians, attempting to deceive them into believing that they are being visited by the real Jesus.

At the time of my dramatic rescue from the New Age movement, I discovered that the masters and the other cunning New Age spirit guides have a leader.

He is, of course, Satan, alias Lucifer, alias the devil.

Long ago the apostle Paul warned us of his deceptive powers: "Satan himself masquerades as an angel of light" (2 Corinthians 11:14).

Chapter 6

Discipleship to a Spirit Guide

What was it like being a disciple of one of Satan's angels? Quite enjoyable, at first. Many fascinating and interesting things began to happen in my life. I was even taken to live in a kind of paradise for a while, and I felt blessed.

I had regarded Djwhal Khul's appearance as a very personal matter and so did not tell anyone about it, not even Muriel.

Several months had passed since the master's visitation. Only a handful of people were in attendance at the midweek healing service held at the Lighted Way. Muriel was conducting the candlelighting ordinance.

A small candle, called the Christ candle, was burning in the center of the altar. Muriel invited each person, in turn, to come up to the altar, take a small white candle, and light it from the burning candle. The person then placed his lighted candle in a circle around the Christ candle. After that Muriel channeled the person a short message.

It was soon my turn to walk forward.

Standing before the altar, I waited for her to give me a personal message. Muriel closed her eyes and channeled: "You are a personal disciple of Djwhal Khul. He is giving you instructions through your meditations and is also implanting thoughtforms into your mind during sleep."

She squinted as if focusing on more data coming into her mind. "In a past lifetime you were a monk in Djwhal Khul's lamasery in Tibet. In your spirit existence before you incarnated into this present life, you had a meeting with him on the spirit planes."

I leaned forward to listen very carefully.

"A pact was made, and you agreed to incarnate with the specific purpose of becoming one of his disciples. It was planned that you would undergo strict training and then help Djwhal Khul in some special projects that needed to be carried out on the planet in connection with the New Age."

Muriel opened her eyes and smiled. With a motion of her hands, she briefly swept my aura in the area of my head and shoulders to balance the energy.

"Thank you," I said, and returned to my seat.

I thought to myself, So Muriel knows about my discipleship. I wonder what else the masters have told her about me.

Because I was determined to be a diligent disciple for my master, I spent a lot of my spare time studying Djwhal Khul's teachings as presented in the Alice Bailey books. I was especially interested in information concerning "the Christ" and his "second coming."

The books stated that the New Age will set the stage for the return of "the Christ," a physical appearance of the master who heads the Hierarchy of Masters. The work of the Hierarchy is to prepare the way for this event; humanity's duty is to accept him and work in harmony with his teachings and advice when he appears.

I learned that the term "the Christ" does not refer to a specific person; rather, it is the name of an executive office within the Hierarchy, equivalent to saying, "the president" of a country. Alice Bailey states that a master called Lord Maitreya holds the position of the Christ, having occupied it for some 2,000 years. She emphasizes that the return of "the Christ" will be the same event as the promised return of the Messiah of Christianity.

Muriel taught the theory that, coinciding with the start of the new age of Aquarius, Maitreya may soon move on to other duties of a more exalted kind elsewhere in the universe. His position as the Christ would, in that case, be taken over by one of the other senior masters, such as Koot Hoomi or "Master Jesus."

She emphasized that the masters need human disciples to help them prepare the planet for the coming of the Christ. The New Age movement is meant to provide a human resource base from which the masters can recruit disciples to work in the various aspects of their operations, areas such as politics, education, religion, culture, commerce, and finance.

To train such disciples, Muriel started the Lighted Way classes in meditation and channeling. The Hierarchy needed dedicated channels who would follow the masters' instructions and would sacrifice time, energy, and money to obediently carry out the directions given—directions that were to be regarded as being the will of God.

In contrast to the process occurring at the Lighted Way, the Bailey writings state that most of the Hierarchy's disciples are unconscious of the relationship they have with their masters. When the master communicates ideas by means of telepathy, the disciple is not even aware of what is happening; he simply thinks the ideas are his own mind's creativity at work. Supposedly many of the world's government leaders, economists, philanthropists, and religious leaders are such "unknowing" disciples of the masters.

"It is time to move out of this house," the inner voice of conscience spoke as I meditated one morning. "I want you to live alone. You need to be in a less distracting home environment, where you can spend more time meditating and studying."

The message came through very clearly. I was still living in the Los Angeles house that I had shared with three close friends for a couple of years. I wondered where I was supposed to move. The inner voice spoke again.

"You should move to the city of Torrance. Find a quiet apartment that has plenty of light. You will be paying more for rent, but do not be concerned. Know that you are blessed by God, and all will be well."

Torrance is a Los Angeles suburb about twenty-five miles south of where I was living. I would be nearer to my job, but I didn't like the idea of living on my own as a recluse. I decided that the direction to move was coming from my higher self and it was in my best interest to obey, even though I was apprehensive.

As I thought about the move, I realized that my lifestyle had changed dramatically since I began attending classes at the Lighted Way and since I became a disciple of Djwhal Khul. My spiritually oriented life was no longer compatible with the worldly "secular" lifestyle of my roommates. I had lost all interest in visiting bars, one of my favorite former pastimes. I had no longer dated since the time I took a private vow of celibacy. As I became aware of how much lurid filth, sexually stimulating material, and violence were depicted in the media, I had gradually decreased attendance at movies. I even made a conscious effort to eliminate all profanities and coarse expressions from my speech as I strove to live as godly a life as I could.

Instead of dating and indulging in "worldly" entertainment, I endeavored to spend my time in the study of esoteric literature, in prayer, and in meditation. Countryside walks and visits to museums replaced visits to the beach and parties. Aspiring to seek after the kingdom of God instead of the things of this world, I spent much time contemplating my spiritual path and walk with "God."

After moving the last of my belongings, I sat on the carpeted floor of my new apartment and meditated. "Welcome to the White Brotherhood," a crisp, clear inner voice announced. "The masters are very pleased with your progress along the path. You are to be congratulated for your willingness to proceed onward in the face of difficulties. Keep moving forward. Keep on the straight and narrow path. You have a tendency to work too hard sometimes. Take time for rest. Keep balanced. My blessings. I am Sanat Kumara."

Wow, I thought, Sanat Kumara himself has taken the time to channel a special message for me. I was amazed how clear the words were, as if someone had actually spoken into the inside of my brain. I was filled with joy and gladness.

From Djwhal Khul's teachings, I was somewhat familiar with Sanat Kumara, a mysterious and interesting character. Apparently all the senior masters of the Hierarchy, including "the Christ," were supervised by this great spirit being of nonhuman origin who supposedly originated from Venus.

My meditations were now always accompanied by bright light shining in my forehead. Muriel told me the light indicated that my third-eye center—the chakra located in the forehead—had been "opened."

Especially after Djwhal Khul's visitation, I noticed that my meditations were sometimes accompanied by mystical phenomena. For example, on several occasions a bright, multicolored display of lights cascaded around inside my forehead. It was like looking into a giant kaleidoscope. On infrequent occasions, I had more profound mystical experiences. One time I woke up in the middle of the night to find my bedroom filled with green light. It looked as if my room were filled with microscopic smoke particles, and a green-colored fluorescent light had been switched on—a bit like a disco filled with colored smoke. In spite of the strangeness of the occurrence, I felt a soothing peace. I had not taken any drugs, for they were forbidden to those on the metaphysical path.

On one Christmas morning, when I sat down to meditate, suddenly my brain was flooded with bright, white light. I felt a beautiful sense of tranquility, like pure bliss. A comforting sensation of warmth filled my body, as if I were sitting in the warm summer sun and the sunshine were able to penetrate the entire depth of my body tissues. Sitting in this peaceful light for several minutes, I thought to myself, What a wonderful Christmas gift from God.

During one Sunday morning worship service, Muriel channeled a prophetic message for me during the candlelighting ordinance.

"Someone at your work is going to leave shortly," she said. "It means that you will be promoted and have more responsibility."

As soon as Muriel spoke, in my own mind I could distinctly hear the name, Jack Thompson. But then I immediately rationalized that there was no way he would leave the company because he had been there so long. I decided that our vice-president must be the person implied in the message.

Two days later, our company president announced an unexpected staff meeting. He began to speak: "I have brought you together to inform you that Jack Thompson is leaving the company."

A chill ran down my spine.

"Jack is moving back to his home state of Missouri," the boss continued. "We wish him all the best in his new venture. We will, of course, need to reorganize the department to cover his duties."

I was shocked. Muriel's message had been absolutely accurate. Furthermore, when Muriel had given me the prophecy, the inner voice of my higher self had clearly told me the correct identity of the person about to leave, even though my rational intelligence had dismissed it as being illogical. I realized that I needed to pay much closer attention to the inner voice of my conscience; apparently it knew information that my rational mind was incapable of accessing.

After Jack's resignation from the company, I received the promotion, just as Muriel had predicted. My trust in Muriel's relationship with "God" was now unshakable, and I was totally dedicated to work with her as part of my discipleship training. I began to entertain the idea that if I obediently followed the discipleship path, I could take the "initiations" talked about in the Bailey writings. Supposedly, these rare events occurred while a disciple was asleep and visiting the heavenly realms in his "soul body." The teachings stated that the ultimate goal of discipleship was to take the fifth initiation, called the "Christhood" initiation. At this, the disciple would become a master himself and live in bliss as an immortal servant of "God."

A few months after Muriel's accurate prophecy regarding the changes at my work, she suddenly suspended the Sunday morning services at the Lighted Way in order to give herself more time for personal transformation. To keep up my rhythm of church going, I was impressed to attend the church nearest to where I lived, which happened to be a Lutheran congregation. Believing that I was walking with the same God, I was happy to worship alongside Christians in their churches.

It was early December. New services and classes had begun at the Lighted Way. During the first Sunday service, Muriel channeled a message for me as I stood at the altar.

"There is going to be a surprise for you at Christmas," she said. No more information was given, and I returned to my seat.

Since joining the Lighted Way, my life had been full of interesting surprises. They were almost becoming the norm, so I didn't pay much attention to this latest message.

Just before Christmas, I knelt in front of the altar in my apartment to begin a session of prayer and meditation. There I received a clear message spoken by the inner voice of the silence. "You are soon going to be making a move that will take you overseas," it said. "Just where you are going is not to be made known yet."

I felt strange. An intuitive sense told me that this message was very important, even though I was not told where or when I would move.

I wondered whether I was going to move back to my home country of England. I also thought that perhaps the masters wanted me to move to Hawaii, where I had been involved with a lot of business dealings in my job.

The next evening, I attended a group channeling session. A partner channeled a personal message for me in response to questions I asked about the impending move. "The move you are to make is not necessarily a permanent one," she said. "It will clear up old energies. It also involves further training under the supervision of the Hierarchy. Start to sell all the things you are not able to take with you. Travel very light. You are entering a new cycle of your life. After this cycle is over, you will be ready to start your soul's true vocation for this incarnation."

It had to be England; my thoughts were constantly focused there. Conflicting feelings swept over me. I was very excited about returning, but I was also apprehensive. I would be leaving a good, secure job to face an unknown future. I agreed to trust the masters and follow their directions.

I prayed this prayer of dedication to "God": "Thank you, Lord, for all your blessings. Thank you for revealing yourself to me. I ask that my life will be guided by your divine power. I ask that all illusions be dispelled from my mind and that your true will be revealed to me. I ask to be used as a servant of the Hierarchy. Amen."

Seeking her advice and approval regarding the apparent move to England, I went to Muriel for a private counseling session. She channeled, "Your life is blessed. Have faith in God and go forth with an attitude of lightness and joy. Though you will be doing various things in England, the move is mainly a pilgrimage to release old attachments and resolve past conflicts with your parents."

Muriel was silent for a few moments before continuing, "I do not see you working in a permanent job. You will do some things for the Hierarchy there. I see you visiting Findhorn."

I quit my job, sold all my furniture, gave away a lot of my belongings, and flew to the United Kingdom with a single suitcase containing all my possessions.

I felt sick with apprehension regarding the move to London. The disorientation from not knowing where I was to stay or what I was to do permeated my entire being. I booked into a hotel and waited for further instructions from the masters.

A few days after my arrival in England, I awoke one morning feeling overwhelmed and depressed. Almost in tears, I decided to seek comfort in meditation. After I sat still for a few moments, suddenly a blast of energy hit me. It felt as if I were being electrocuted as a surge of light blitzed through my entire body and the voice of "God" howled into my inner ear, "Go forth in strength!"

If I had not been sitting in a chair, the force of the energy may well have knocked me to the floor. The blast lasted for just a couple of seconds. After a pause of a couple more seconds, the energy blast hit me again.

"Go forth in strength!" the voice repeated.

I was then slain a third time.

"Go forth in strength!" it blitzed.

Then there was silence.

It was reassuring to know that "God" was helping me. I felt at peace. My faith had been activated again, and I went forward with courage.

Feeling that I should stay in London, I rented a small

apartment in the Earl's Court district. I had absolutely no idea how long I would be staying there or what I was supposed to be doing. Perhaps it is a permanent move, I thought. I will assume it is until I receive directions informing me otherwise.

After the miraculous blast of energy from "God," I hoped that my medical problems would be healed. Unfortunately, I was to be disappointed. My ailments remained. Only my courage and faith had been boosted by the display of "God's" power.

During the day, I mainly looked for a job. In the evenings I was impressed to take part in the activities of several New Age organizations. I cherished a visit I made to the London operations of the Lucis Trust, the organization that publishes Djwhal Khul's Alice Bailey books.

On Sunday mornings I attended services at a local Anglican church. Sadness and disappointment filled me as I observed how small the congregations in England were compared to the size of the churches. Religion had been in decline for years, with many church buildings derelict or converted into warehouses. Secularism had taken over. I regarded the New Age as being the new hope to fill the spiritual void.

One morning in meditation, I was instructed to make a pilgrimage to the famous Canterbury Cathedral, mother church of the worldwide Anglican denomination. I had a beautiful time in Canterbury and spent the entire day visiting that great historic church with its massive arches and stone walls. Meditating in the sanctuary, I recited occult prayers and invocations and performed an imagery ritual, in which I visualized the cathedral and all its daughter churches being filled with the "Christ light" channeled by the Hierarchy of Masters.

I made visits to several other great cathedrals. On each occasion, I spent time meditating and praying in the sanctuary, finishing the session with occult invocations and metaphysical imagery rituals.

Vatican City of the New Age movement. This is how Findhorn has been described. Upon arrival, I was absolutely overwhelmed by the community of almost 400 people, located in a beautiful part of the Scottish Highlands. Here, Satan has built a paradise for his New Age followers.

The inner voice of meditation told me to visit this New Age mecca about six months after my arrival in England. I had only a vague recollection that Findhorn was some kind of small Christian retreat center located in northern Scotland. Muriel had channeled that I would visit Findhorn, but I had actually forgotten all about her prophecy since leaving the United States.

Packing my bags, I drove all the way up to the northern part of Scotland, where I had located the village of Findhorn on a map. I anticipated staying at Findhorn for perhaps a couple of days. The Masters had other plans.

This New Age Vatican City began in 1962 as a small vacation trailer housing three adults and three children. From this humble beginning, Satan worked a miracle in building up his prime New Age educational institution.

The commune now comprises of a large mobile home and trailer park with extensive gardens and community buildings, an eighty-seven room hotel that looks like a beautiful castle, a gorgeous auditorium with facilities for performing arts classes, a publishing house with printing shop, and several stately mansions complete with extensive gardens. The community has hosted international conferences, and many thousands of visitors have poured through its doors to attend its residential educational programs.

This community is not a bunch of hippies. Most of the people I met were university-educated professionals. During my stay, I made friends with a former Jesuit priest, a seminary professor, and several psychologists, to list but a few.

The main tenet of Findhorn's philosophy is the idea that a "Christ energy" or "Christ-consciousness" resides within each person. If people meditate, they can have access to this infinite source of "wisdom" inside themselves known as the "Christ-self," or higher self. The goal of Findhorn's teachings is to train people to attune to the "Christ" within and use it to guide their lives.

What I originally thought was going to be a two-day visit soon became a two-month venture with no sign that I should leave. My meditation "guidance" kept telling me to stay at the community and participate in the long-term guest programs. These involved working for departments within the community.

For most of the time, I worked for the publications department, helping to publish and manufacture the various New Age books, magazines, and brochures printed by the Findhorn Press. These included such books as David Spangler's *Reflections Upon the Christ* and Donald Keys's *Earth at Omega*, a book advocating the idea of a single world government as the means of transforming the world and solving the critical problems it faces. Keys is the founder of Planetary Citizens, a worldwide New Age organization seeking change through political action. He has been a long-time consultant to the United Nations.

The supervisor of guest workers in publications was a charming elderly woman who had been living at Findhorn for many years. She once confided to me that she was a Christian and regarded Jesus Christ as her master. I became acquainted with other community members who had at one time been Bible teachers; one of them was a former priest. Apparently, somewhere along their Christian path they took a wrong turn.

As part of a two-month-long orientation program designed to integrate people into full membership of the commune, I was required to have an interview with two members of the community's personnel department. This was to help them decide if I could be accepted as a full member. After I had explained my situation and answered their questions, the three of us did a group meditation. During the meditation, an intense, bright light shone in my forehead. The energy was so strong that the couch I sat on seemed to vibrate. This gave me confidence that my application to become a full member was in "divine" order.

Jay, a bearded Canadian of slim build, was the head of the personnel department. He started to speak during the meditation. "In the best interest of Will's higher self, what advice can be given?" He seemed to be asking the spirit world for guidance.

A further period of silence followed. In my own mind I heard the words, "Yes, it is in divine order to join."

Jay closed the meditation and confirmed that he received a positive sense that it was God's will for me to become a member.

I began to see my role in life as becoming a type of priest. I rejected my past aspirations—professional success, financial comfort, and social standing—and accepted a new image of humbly working for God in the role of a New Age monk, living a life of simplicity and doing good deeds. I pledged myself to work for the uplifting of humanity through selfless service.

I was allowed to join the publications staff as a full member of the community. I was very happy to be a member of the world's foremost New Age organization and looked forward to the wonderful opportunity of working for the masters.

Excruciating despair swept over me.

I had just awakened in the morning and mysteriously "knew" I had to leave Findhorn and return to Los Angeles. The sudden, totally unexpected news devastated me. I had been a full member of the community for only one week.

Don't ask me how I knew, but it was clear to me that my time at Findhorn was over and that the masters wanted me to return to the Lighted Way. It was as if the idea to leave had been implanted in my brain while I was asleep.

I recalled reading that the masters have the ability to plant "thoughtforms" into the mind of a disciple during sleep. When the disciple awakens, these thoughtforms, manifested as powerful ideas, demand attention and action. I reasoned that a thoughtform must have been implanted in my mind that night.

I had come to appreciate living at Findhorn. I had made many friends and did not want to leave such a paradise. After living in the beautiful Scottish Highlands for six months, I dreaded returning to smoggy, congested Los Angeles and its rat race.

Eventually pulling myself out of bed, I dressed and headed for the sanctuary. A lot of meditating needed to be done before I was willing to give up my beloved home.

Over the next few days, I spent hours and hours in the sanctuary in silent contemplation. For some reason, I felt nauseated with worry and apprehension at the prospect of returning to Los Angeles. But the inner voice of meditation continually confirmed the need to move. I finally reasoned that if I wanted to continue serving my beloved master, then I had no choice but to obey the direction given.

What will Jay in personnel think? I wondered. I had just given him a commitment to stay at Findhorn for at least a year. Because the inner voice of my higher self would not allow me to tell people that I was a personal disciple of Djwhal Khul, I had to come up with a plausible explanation for my abrupt change of plan.

I approached Jay with embarrassment as he stood in line for communal dinner. "Jay, I have some bad news for you. I have to leave the community."

Jay replied, "Oh. Well, I'm not surprised really. Why don't you come and see me tomorrow?"

Fortunately, he understood my predicament of having received unexpected guidance from "God." I was able to leave with integrity intact and an open door to return in the future.

Two years later I did return for a visit—as an unusual born-again Christian with a gospel message of salvation through Jesus.

Chapter 7

Taken to the Limit

"Muriel," I asked, "why did the masters want me to leave Findhorn and return to Los Angeles?"

Having flown into town the previous day, I was having a private counseling session with Muriel at the Lighted Way. Muriel used psychological and spiritual counseling as a means of financially supporting the work of the metaphysical center. Most of the clients were not regular students at the Lighted Way. Some people came for serious psychotherapy, others for psychic readings or healings.

Muriel channeled: "The masters wanted you to visit Findhorn, but not to stay there permanently. Because they knew you would like it there, they arranged a test of your obedience; they also wanted you to learn and grow through experiencing other lifestyles."

Muriel was not in a meditation state, but had been channeling with her eyes wide open as if in normal conversation. Apparently her years of practice had enabled her to channel while in normal, everyday consciousness.

She continued: "In coming back, you have experienced much growth and development in maturity and understanding. You feel a strong urge now to want to help others."

Listening intently, I mentally agreed with what she said.

"The New Age cannot be just groups of people living in remote communes," she explained. "These retreats are good, but they are not the New Age. Our way is to fully integrate into the world and bring light into it. Integrating is a more difficult path than living in a retreat. The masters want you in Los Angeles to help pioneer the path of being in the world, but not of the world."

After a pause, I asked with concern, "Should I try to return to my old job?"

"Know that you are blessed by 'God,' " she replied. "Doors will open. Go and see your old boss. If it is in God's will, things will work out with him."

My former boss was pleased to see me. After some thought, he offered me a job, and I began commercial employment again.

As I resumed attending classes at the Lighted Way, I noticed a change in the emphasis of Muriel's teachings. Instead of focusing upon channeling the masters, she now channeled "the Father." The change was subtle, but the teachings had a much more devotional and religious flavor than the former intellectual metaphysical teachings.

Muriel claimed that she had undergone a certain initiation that enabled her to channel "the Father" directly. In the groups, we began to spend time praying to "the Father," almost as one would in a Christian church. The channelings were even cloaked in language similar to that in the King James Version of the Bible. During one of the light circle channeling sessions, a student channeled the following message: "When you wake up in the morning and start the day, first go to the Father in prayer and ask him, 'Father, what wilt thou have me do this day to glorify thy name?' "

The channeling left a deep impression on me. The following morning I set up a small altar in my apartment. On the top of the altar I placed two silver candlesticks containing tall white candles. The altar also had an incense holder on it. After lighting the candles and incense, I knelt before the altar and prayed, "Father, what wilt thou have me do this day to glorify thy name?"

I then meditated and opened myself to any instructions that "the Father" may have had for me. I decided that each morning I would start my period of devotional prayer and meditation with this invocation to "the Father."

One evening, I went to bed as usual. Closing my eyes, I suddenly felt soothing energy filling my entire body. As I opened my eyes again, I saw that the bedroom was filled with green light, as if a green arc lamp had been switched on to fill the room with light.

I concluded that the masters must be sending light into the room. I tried to fall asleep but was unable to do so. Every time I opened my eyes, the room was still filled with the green light. Feeling a deep serenity and sense of peace, I did not sleep one wink all night.

Expecting to feel quite tired at work the next day, I was surprised to discover I had plenty of energy, just as if I had had an excellent night's sleep.

The next night, exactly the same thing occurred. I did not sleep at all, but felt peaceful tranquility as my bedroom was filled with light. Again the mystical light— this time blue—was present all night long.

In the morning I felt perfectly rested. I worked hard all day at my job, had plenty of energy, and felt alert, in spite of the fact that I had not had a single second of sleep during two consecutive nights.

At the next class, I asked Muriel what she thought had been happening to me.

"Angels were attending you and giving you healing energy," she stated, as if channeling the information.

Unfortunately, I could not see any effects of this "healing" energy upon my health problems; my ailments were still fully evident. I reasoned that perhaps remission of my symptoms would occur later, but was disappointed when no healing occurred. In fact, the longer I was associated with the New Age movement, the worse my health became—in spite of the numerous "healings" I had received from Muriel and other New Age healers during special healing services and other private appointments.

Several months later Muriel phoned me unexpectedly while I was at my desk at work. "Last night the Father awakened me," she reported. "He spoke to me and told me that we will need six thousand dollars in order to prepare new lesson materials and start an intensive advertising thrust to promote new classes at the Lighted Way. The Father instructed me to call up the disciples and ask them for contributions toward this project."

Without giving much thought to what had been said, I replied, "Well, Muriel, let me see what I can do."

During our Sunday morning services, I had always given at least a twenty-dollar offering. On several occasions I gave a generous one-hundred-dollar donation. However, this was the first time that Muriel had ever spoken to me directly and asked for special donations to support the activity of the Lighted Way.

After work, I went to a nearby automatic teller machine to check how much money I had available in my account. There was just over five hundred dollars— all the money I had in the world. My trip to England and the stay at Findhorn had depleted all of my savings.

Having strong faith in the ability of "God" to take care of all my financial needs, I decided to immediately send Muriel a check for five hundred dollars. It was all the money I had; what more could I do? I did not even meditate on the matter. I simply wrote out a check and put it in the mail. I was happy to be a child of "God" and know I was under the special care and protection of my master. I had total trust in Djwhal Khul and his ability to help me wisely plan my life and obtain whatever resources I needed.

Two days later, I awoke with an uneasy feeling inside. A powerful thought in my mind indicated that I needed to send another five hundred dollars to Muriel immediately.

I got up and proceeded to carry out my morning meditation. I began with prayer and said, "Father, what wilt thou have me do this day to glorify thy name?"

"Send another five hundred dollars," the inner voice of my higher self confirmed.

I didn't feel good about this answer, knowing I had no more money left. But when I reviewed my finances, I discovered that, with my payroll check going into the bank the following day, I would have just sufficient funds available to cover the check. I concluded that this was a time when sacrifices were needed, even though I felt uneasy about cutting my finances so close.

After I dropped the check in a local mailbox, I noticed the uneasy feeling lifted, as if a release had occurred in my nervous system in response to my obeying the inner direction.

I had known Muriel for more than four years, and she had told me that since the time she originally started the Lighted Way some twenty years before, she had used up all of her personal resources in order to support the ongoing expenses of operating the center. She once told me that she had even sold her house in order to pay for the work of the masters. Her sacrifice had been tremendous.

Knowing that Muriel had been brought up in a relatively wealthy and cultured family, I realized it must have been very difficult for her to ask me for money, even though the funds were to be used to finance the work of the Hierarchy. I had absolutely no doubt that Muriel had been specifically directed by her spirit guidance to ask the disciples for special donations.

A couple of days after sending the second donation, a sick feeling filled the pit of my stomach as I awoke. In the front of my mind was the powerful thought that I needed to send more money to Muriel. Intuitively, I was aware that the amount needed was one thousand dollars.

Apprehensively I thought to myself: No, this can't be. I don't have any more money. This idea must be merely rubbish coming from my mind's own nonsense realms.

I decided that I had better do some deep meditating to find out just what was going on. "Father, what wilt thou have me do this day so that I might glorify thy name?" I asked sincerely in prayer.

The morning meditation was confusing. In my emotionally turbulent state I couldn't meditate clearly. So I decided to go to work and meditate further on the matter when I returned home in the evening.

Returning from work, as usual, I lighted candles and incense upon the altar in my apartment. Kneeling down before the altar, I prayed: "Dear heavenly Father, I ask that you will give me clear guidance regarding the financial donations required for the Lighted Way. Please reveal to me clearly if you want me to send a thousand dollars at this time."

I then meditated while still on my knees, holding my hands clasped as in prayer.

The inner voice of conscience quietly spoke to me. "Yes," it said. "You need to send a check for one thousand dollars right away. The money is needed to carry on the work of bringing more people into a knowledge of the New Age. We need more people on the path of discipleship."

In my own thinking, I protested: "How am I supposed to send money when I have nothing left in my bank account?"

The inner voice of meditation replied immediately, "You have credit cards. Use them."

An uncomfortable apprehension flooded over me. The heart chakra area of my back felt very warm.

I then protested that I regarded my credit cards as a source of cash only in an emergency.

"This is an emergency," the inner voice rebuked. "The money is needed now to do my work."

After a few moments of contemplation, I reluctantly

decided to end my resistance and send the money, even though I felt uncomfortable and tense about what was happening.

I made out the check and took it to a mailbox. As I dropped the envelope into the box, my apprehension suddenly disappeared. The anxiety vanished, as if by magic it had been lifted from me.

I now had to transfer funds from my MasterCard account into my checking account to cover the check. Thinking about my finances, I reasoned that realistically I could afford what I had given and would soon be able to pay off the credit card account.

Two days later when I awakened in the morning, a tune was playing in my mind. I could hear the lyrics as clearly as if I were listening to a radio playing through stereo headphones:

> Take it to the limit,
> oh, ho, ho.
> Take it to the limit,
> oh, ho, ho.
> Take it to the limit. . . .

I remembered the song to have been a hit pop number several years previously. Accompanying the tune was a powerful thought that I needed to send another thousand-dollar check to Muriel. In my imagination, I could clearly see a check with $1,000 written on it. Horror filled the pit of my stomach. "Oh, no! When is this thing going to end?" I exclaimed to myself.

Climbing out of bed, I thought: Don't panic; maybe the idea of donating more money is just emotional nonsense. Surely "God" would not want me to go into debt, not when I have zero assets to my name. I tried to stay calm and objective. Maybe this time the masters were just joking around.

As I showered, the song still ran through my mind.

> Take it to the limit,
> Oh, take it to the limit,
> la, la, la
> Take it to the limit,
> oh, oh, oh
> Take it to the limit. . . .

I felt depressed and terribly frustrated about the whole situation and decided not to send any money at this time. All day at work the song kept playing in my mind, over and over and over again. I had never sung this song to myself before; it wasn't even my type of music, although I could remember the number playing on jukeboxes in the bars I had frequented years before.

Deciding that I was not prepared to go into debt to finance Muriel's center, I refused to send any more money. Besides, I sometimes had reservations about the things Muriel said. I had wondered if all of her messages and directions really came from a "divine" source. I suspected that one or two strange channelings may have come from astral entities.[1] Sometimes Muriel said things that just did not seem to square with what had been written by Djwhal Kuhl in the Bailey books. Sometimes she said things that just didn't feel right. I considered my decision not to send more money to be final.

Although my mind was made up, my decision did not affect the way I felt. Severe depression began to build inside me. It was almost as if I were under a spell of oppression. The lyrics "take it to the limit . . ." were constantly bombarding my mind. No matter what I did, I could not erase these words from my mind. They were there when I ate, when I spoke on the phone, when I

---

1. Metaphysics postulates that there are low-intelligence entities existing on the lower levels of the spirit realms, or astral planes. These entities include fairies, hobgoblins, and ghosts. It is claimed that sometimes a channeler can accidentally receive messages from these mischievous astral beings.

used my computer, and when I tried to deliberately sing a different song.

Hounding commands accompanied the lyrics.

"You have to send the money," the voice of conscience blasted.

"One thousand dollars," it repeated.

Arriving home after work, I meditated. The inner voice sternly rebuked, "You must send the money. Send it now!"

For once, I did not want to listen to my higher self. I wished it to be silenced. But it was relentless.

> Take it to the limit,
> oh, ho, ho.
> Send it; send the check.
> One thousand dollars.
> Take it to the limit,
> la, la, la.

Getting down on my knees before the altar, I prayed to "God." "Dear heavenly Father, deeply I come before you and pray that you will bring me wisdom and clarity of mind. I do not want to do anything foolish. Please show me clearly what you want me to do in regard to financially supporting the Lighted Way. I ask that I am aligned to your will and that you will protect me from all false and astral influences."

After a pause to meditate, I continued the prayer. "Father, I really mean it when each day I start my meditation with the words 'What wilt thou have me do this day?' "

"Use your MasterCard!" the voice thundered.

I thought, How far is this going to go?

"I also want you to immediately apply for credit-limit increases," the voice interjected.

A cold shiver shot down my spine.

"Don't worry. You will be blessed in what you are doing," the higher self assured. "The Father is with you."

I felt awful. The sickly depression intensified. I perceived I was resisting the will of "God."

I thought to myself, If I send this one thousand dollars, will the masters then want me to give even more?

I decided I had better get the check written. I couldn't stand the tension, anxiety, and depression any longer. The lyrics of the song were driving me crazy.

As I wrote out the check, I wondered whether the severe depression resulted from separation from God caused by my disobedience.

I drove over to the mail-deposit box. As soon as I dropped the envelope into the box, the sickly depression lifted instantly. I also noticed that the music in my head had gone. In the welcome silence, I felt "normal" again.

When I woke up the next morning, the first thing I did was check out my mind. Nothing unusual was there. No powerful thoughtforms were telling me to make further donations. I breathed a big sigh of relief.

About a week passed in relative peace. Then one early morning I woke up with a new idea implanted in my mind. I needed to immediately donate two thousand dollars to the Lighted Way.

"Oh, no! Not again!" I protested in anger.

I hesitantly climbed out of bed and took a shower. As I was showering, suddenly the music and words, "Take it to the limit, oh, oh, oh. . . ." burst into my mind. The music and the words were as clear as if I wore headphones connected to a cassette. Hearing every note in stereo was an amazing, but horrifying experience.

"What should I do now?" I asked myself loudly.

There was no answer. All I could hear was the song. "Take it to the limit. . . ."

After dressing, I fell down on my knees in front of the altar.

As I meditated, the imagery of meditation now pictured a check with a figure of $3,000 written on it. Thinking to myself that three thousand dollars was ludicrous, I decided to immediately write a check for two thousand dollars without any further resistance or protest. I was not prepared to resist any longer and risk going through all that terrible depression again. If the Hierarchy wanted a further one thousand dollars, they could have it. The pain of resisting was not worth it. It was better to just do what they wanted and get it over with.

I reasoned that the masters knew what they were doing; they would just have to help me pay back all the accumulated debt. It was useless to resist.

After sending the check for two thousand dollars, I transferred funds from my Visa account into my checking account to prevent the check from bouncing. What a relief not to feel any more anxiety that day. It was better to obey than put up useless resistance against the will of "God."

I believed that through my obedience I was building for myself a place in the kingdom of "God" and that I would be blessed with rewards of joy and abundance on account of every penny I spent on "God's" precious work.

The next morning, sure enough, the song was there again. "Take it to the limit, one more time."

I intuitively knew a thousand dollars was needed.

The emphasis of the song's words was now on the final phrase, "one more time." I wondered if the emphasis indicated that this check would be my last donation.

The inner voice explained, "You should have sent the full three thousand dollars, just as you were instructed yesterday. Send the outstanding one thousand dollars right now."

I wrote out the check without resistance. That check brought my total donation over the two-week period to a total of six thousand dollars, the very amount Muriel had asked for.

The music did not return, perhaps because my credit cards had been taken to their credit limit.

At this stage in my New Age experience, I was becoming totally "possessed" by the spirit demons. I had little ability to resist their telepathic manipulation of my emotions and control of my conscience. Some incredible changes were soon to take place in my life.

Chapter 8

The New Age Center Studies the Bible

"The Father has revealed to me that the Bible contains great wisdom and power," Muriel announced at the beginning of the new series of discipleship training classes. With curiosity, I had noticed the Bible on her lap as she sat at the front of our small group.

"He has directed me to start Bible study here at the Lighted Way," she continued. "In this class we are going to use the Bible as our main reference book."

I was surprised to hear Muriel's announcement. I didn't think our New Age center would ever study the old Bible.

Muriel opened the large, leather-bound Bible. "I am reading from the gospel of Mark," she said. "In chapter eleven, verse twenty-four, Jesus is speaking about faith and the power of prayer. He says, 'Therefore I tell you, whatever you ask for in prayer, believe that you have received it, and it will be yours.' "

Leaning down, Muriel placed the Bible on the carpet beside her chair and then followed the scripture reading with a dissertation on the verse quoted. She emphasized that, when one goes to the Father in prayer with a certain request, it is important to believe that you have already received what you are asking for.

"If, for example, you pray for a healing," she explained, "right after you have prayed, you need to believe that you have been healed, even though the symptoms have not yet disappeared."

I felt a little strange sitting in this first Bible-study class. I had always been enthusiastic about studying Djwhal Khul's writings and about Muriel's channelings of the masters. But for some reason I was hesitant about getting involved with Bible teachings. Since joining the New Age movement, I had regarded the Bible to be very much out of date.

After Muriel's talk, we did some group meditation work and took turns praying to the "Father" that the work at the Lighted Way would be blessed. We also offered prayers for our personal needs.

Jesus Christ Appears and Performs a Healing

During a subsequent class at the Lighted Way, Muriel excitedly told us about a wonderful experience that had recently happened to her.

"While staying at the Brentwood Holiday Inn, I was awakened in the middle of the night. To my amazement, a man stood right in the middle of my hotel bedroom."

Muriel opened her mouth wide and raised her eyebrows, mimicking an expression of astonishment.

She continued: "I was shocked to see him standing there in front of me. He was about six feet tall and had a dignified bearing of great authority. He said to me, 'Get down on your knees!' "

Muriel paused, as if to catch her breath. My eyes were firmly glued on her. "He spoke again, very firmly, and said, 'Get down on your knees. I am Jesus Christ, and I am going to heal you.' That is exactly what he said. I was overwhelmed by the force of his presence."

Muriel said she got out of bed and knelt down in front of the mysterious stranger. She described the person who stood before her.

"Jesus was very handsome. He had the decisive quality of a powerful businessman or distinguished politician. Yet he had a certain ease and charisma that was indicative of his divinity and great wisdom. If people think that Jesus is a weedy weakling, they are going to be surprised."

Even though I found Muriel's story amazing, I had no doubts that the event had happened to her just as she described. Having known Muriel for several years, I had developed a very trusting relationship with her.

"He is power-r-r-ful," she expressed forcefully. "He touched my head with his hands. After blessing me, he walked straight through the solid, locked door of my hotel room and disappeared into the corridor."

After the miraculous visit by "Jesus Christ" to Muriel, the Lighted Way began to change considerably, taking on a much more Christian atmosphere.

My entire philosophical orientation seemed to be threatened by these new Bible teachings, and I began to feel uncomfortable. However, I reasoned that Master Jesus was, after all, a senior master in the Hierarchy; it was thus quite in order for us to study what he taught as recorded in the Bible.

From the Bailey books, I recalled that Master Jesus was responsible for the supervision of all Christianity. Respecting his position as one of the great masters, I concluded that perhaps it would be useful to become acquainted with his teachings. They could aptly supplement the metaphysical knowledge I had learned from Djwhal Khul's dissertations.

In one Bible-study class, Muriel lectured on the use of Jesus' name in prayer. Reading from the Bible, Muriel quoted the words of Jesus. "I will do whatever you ask in my name, so that the Son may bring glory to the Father. You may ask me for anything in my name, and I will do it" (John 14:13, 14).

Muriel commented, "In this text from the Gospel of John, Jesus tells his followers to ask for things in his name. The name of Jesus is the greatest name in the universe, and it should always be invoked when praying."

She looked up at the class in seriousness. "When you pray," she said, "you should address your prayers to the Father, just as Jesus had instructed his disciples when he gave them the example of the Lord's Prayer. However, when you ask for things in prayer, ask for them in Jesus' name. It is the most powerful name that can be used for invocation purposes."

Muriel then told us that she had been instructed by "the Father" to purchase a television and watch TV evangelists, especially Kenneth Copeland and Kenneth Hagin. "I need to study their preaching techniques. He says that, of Christian preachers, they are the nearest to the New Age. The Father wants me to learn from them in order to enhance my own ministry here at the Lighted Way."

Muriel then urged us to begin watching these TV evangelists as much as possible. Because I regarded television in general to be polluted with evil junk, I had not owned a TV set in years and was thus unacquainted with the preachers Muriel was discussing. But I decided to listen to the recommended preachers on my car radio as often as I could.

Jesus Christ Appears to a Guru

With the new emphasis on Jesus Christ at the Lighted Way, an intriguing memory surfaced in my mind. I remembered a visit I had made to a Sunday morning church service held by the Self Realization Fellowship (SRF), a Los Angeles–based Hindu organization.

The service was held in a beautiful chapel located at the organization's Lake Shrine center, about three miles from the site where I attended metaphysical classes at the Lighted Way. What impressed me the most about the SRF chapel was the six large paintings on the front of the altar depicting the historic gurus most closely connected with the organization. One of the two center pictures was of Jesus Christ. At the time, I wondered why this Hindu sect should so highly esteem Jesus

Christ. However, I had not investigated the matter.

With the Lighted Way's emphasis now upon the teachings of Jesus Christ, I was inspired to revisit the SRF chapel and ask the monks questions regarding their relationship to Christianity.

Arriving early, I took a seat in the sanctuary. Soon the chapel filled to capacity for the morning service, and an overflow crowd began to congregate in the large garden, where they listened to the service via loudspeakers.

The program began with sacred songs. The "pastor"—looking like some kind of monk—wore a traditional red Hindu gown. After a short introduction to the sermon, there was a meditation, followed by the rest of the sermon.

The sermon had a curious flavor—a blend of Hindu and Christian teachings—although the Eastern teachings seemed to predominate. The program closed with a prayer in which all the congregation stood and held their arms straight up in the air.

I later questioned one of the senior monks—a balding, flabby man wearing a red jacket styled like a physician's coat. It appeared that the jacket was a uniform worn by monks of the sect.

"Do you believe in the devil?" I asked.

The monk produced a Bible and read several passages to me. I was impressed with his detailed knowledge of the Scriptures. We had an interesting discussion. He recommended I purchase *Autobiography of a Yogi* written by Paramahansa Yogananda, the founder of the organization.

From the book, I learned that Yogananda had been born in India and trained in a Hindu ashram for several years prior to his emigration to America. Yogananda had been sent to the United States by his guru to establish a monastery in the West for the dissemination of Hindu teachings to Westerners. In response to a prophetic dream, Yogananda selected a mansion in Los Angeles as the site for his monastic center.

Near the end of the book, I came across a passage that answered my question about why SRF had such a high regard for Jesus Christ.

> One of the happiest periods of my life was spent in dictating, for *Self Realization Magazine*, my interpretation of part of the New Testament. Fervently I implored Christ to guide me in divining the true meaning of his words, many of which have been grievously misunderstood for twenty centuries.

I was impressed with Yogananda's enthusiasm for the New Testament scriptures. I continued reading his narrative in earnest.

> One night while I was engaged in silent prayer, my sitting room in the Encinitas hermitage became filled with an opal-blue light. I beheld the radiant form of the blessed Lord Jesus. A young man, he seemed, of about twenty-five, with a sparse beard and moustache; his long black hair, parted in the middle, was haloed by a shimmering gold.
>
> His eyes were eternally wondrous; as I gazed, they were infinitely changing. With each divine transition in their expression, I intuitively understood the wisdom conveyed. In his glorious gaze I felt the power that upholds the myriad worlds. A Holy Grail appeared at his mouth; it came down to my lips and then returned to Jesus. After a few moments he uttered beautiful words, so personal in their nature that I keep them in my heart.

In my thinking at the time, I began to appreciate what appeared to be a wonderful connection between the various religions of the world; Jesus had appeared to

Hindus, such as Yogananda, as well to Christians, such as Reverend Hagin. I perceived that all of the different religions were really just part of an emerging divine wholeness, and it was the goal of the New Age to integrate all these diversities of theological thought into one harmonious religion.

The New Age ideal seemed a beautiful concept: to have unity in diversity so as to reveal the fullness of God and produce a society of loving understanding and mutual interdependence. This would be the New Age of love, light, and joy—the kingdom of heaven on earth.

The Kenneth Copeland Convention

Muriel seemed to mention Kenneth Copeland's name almost every time we had a Bible-study class. From the radio broadcasts I heard, this renowned evangelist from Fort Worth, Texas, certainly seemed a very good preacher. However, I remained skeptical about Muriel's assertion that he was inclining toward some of the rudimentary New Age ideas. His programs sounded like 100 percent biblical preaching to me.

While listening to one of Copeland's radio broadcasts, an announcement attracted my attention to an event called the West Coast Believer's Voice of Victory Convention. It was to be held shortly in the Anaheim Convention Center and would feature preaching by Copeland and his leading staff members. I thought that it might be a good idea to attend this event and hear Copeland in person. Perhaps I might discover something about this preacher that I had failed to appreciate while listening to his radio broadcasts.

"Have you registered, sir?" asked the uniformed doorman as I entered the foyer of the convention center's main building. I could already hear singing and shouts of hallelujah coming from inside the arena.

I brushed past him saying, "No, but I am not going to stay long. Thank you."

I didn't want to be bothered with any registration, for I did not plan to stay around long and be bored by some old-fashioned Bible preacher. I was checking Copeland out, mostly in deference to Muriel.

The huge indoor arena contained about 6,000 worshipers. Some of the people wept; others uttered unintelligible words, which I guessed must be the tongues. Some people prayed, some busily looked up Bible texts, others munched on popcorn or gulped down soda drinks as if they were at a baseball game. I had never seen anything like it.

Looking around the arena for a place to sit, I noticed the upper-level rows were empty. "I better sit up there, away from these noisy Christians," I said to myself. "Otherwise, some weird emotional energy might rub off on me." Djwhal Khul taught that emotional energy was not good for someone on the metaphysical path.

Reaching my seat, I watched the proceedings as a detached spectator. A man was singing from the platform. At the end of the song, he started to speak. I realized that it was Kenneth Copeland himself and admitted that he certainly was a gifted artist.

After a short reading from the Bible, Copeland then proceeded with his sermon. He seemed to be an excellent speaker, but, unfortunately, his subject matter was the same old Christian stuff I had heard preached as a youth. He was talking about how to prevent the devil from stealing the joy felt by the Christian.

I wondered why Muriel regarded him as especially inspired by "God" and as having a level of consciousness that inclined toward some of the New Age ideas. I certainly couldn't see it and decided that Muriel was probably mistaken. But to be fair, I would listen a little longer.

I sat waiting for some new, extrabiblical information. I waited and waited. All I heard was old-fashioned sermonizing with a lot of Bible texts thrown in. After half an hour, I was getting rather bored.

I thought to myself, I am glad I came. Now I have proved to myself that this evangelist is not to be taken seriously, after all, even if Muriel is so impressed. In no way could this Bible pusher's knowledge be compared with the vast and intricate metaphysical teachings of Djwhal Khul. It seemed to me that Muriel herself had far more knowledge concerning divine matters than even the most gifted Christian big shots.

Even though I became increasingly bored and felt like walking out and going home, a strange force operating within me seemed to prompt me to stay in my seat. So I sat there and tried to be interested in what the man was saying.

Eventually the boredom became too much for me, and I jumped out of my seat and walked down the flights of stairs. On my way home I thought, Well, that's the last of him. Back to my Alice Bailey books and Muriel's commentaries on the Bible.

In my morning meditation the next day, I received a surprising direction. "Tonight, go back to the Kenneth Copeland convention," the inner voice of conscience advised.

"Hmmm," I said to myself.

I decided to do what I was told. Perhaps the masters wanted me to meet someone there; perhaps Copeland would teach me something after all; perhaps I needed an additional dose of boredom to be absolutely convinced once and for all that the big-time Bible preachers really didn't know that much.

In the early evening, I returned to the convention and sat in the same isolated location as before. Surprisingly, I quite enjoyed the singing, even lifting up my hands at one point. Then Copeland started preaching. I was disappointed again; he just preached more Bible stuff. The more he rapped, the more bored I become.

Finally, I decided to meditate. Pulling myself forward to the edge of the seat, I straightened my back and began the usual occult visualizations, incantations, and invocations. After about twenty minutes, I closed the meditation by visualizing "Christ energy" filling the arena.

After the meditation, I was impressed to stay until the end of the evening's program. Eventually Copeland finished, and I returned home, convinced that this was my last visit.

This was not to be. The following morning in my meditation, I was shocked to be told that I should again attend the convention in the evening after work. I recalled the old proverb "Ours is not to question why; ours is but to do or die."

After work, I drove the thirty miles to the convention and went straight to my "usual" seat.

As Copeland was preaching, suddenly something he said riveted my attention. A chill ran up my spine as I involuntarily slid to the edge of my seat to focus on his words.

I heard him describe how he had recently been given a vision from God. I heard Copeland say that God had told him that Jesus would soon begin to appear in a physical form in the churches. Jesus, perhaps accompanied by his angels, would be seen walking down the aisles and then would disappear. This would occur in several churches with increasing frequency.

The statement I heard was like dynamite in my ears. Wow, I thought, this is interesting. Muriel had predicted exactly the same thing. She had recently told us at the Lighted Way that we could expect Jesus to appear during our church service.

In fact, I recalled that Muriel had also made a very similar prediction about four years previously. On that occasion, the prediction concerned the masters of the Hierarchy. The Hierarchy had informed Muriel that certain senior masters, such as Saint Germain, Koot Hoomi, or Djwhal Khul, would materialize themselves in a physical form and be seen in the Lighted Way, perhaps sitting quietly for a few minutes in one of the seats during our Sunday morning metaphysical church service.

The appearance of the masters was to be part of the "externalization of the Hierarchy." This is supposedly a process in which the members of the Hierarchy appear in visual, physical form in the world in order to promote the New Age teachings in a more dynamic manner than before.

As I sat at the convention, I concluded that Muriel was correct in her assessment of Kenneth Copeland as a preacher inspired by Master Jesus. It appeared he was at least expressing some New Age ideas. I recalled that on an earlier radio broadcast, Ken Copeland claimed it was possible to receive "revelation knowledge" directly from God through the power of the Holy Spirit. It certainly appeared he had received special knowledge.

I started to get excited; perhaps the Hierarchy really were working through some of the Christian evangelists, after all, just as Muriel claimed. Feeling much more accommodating toward Christian believers, I wondered whether other preachers were being directly influenced by the Hierarchy, even if the preachers themselves were not consciously aware of the source of their inspiration.

At the end of the meeting, I left the arena and drove home along the freeway with the words and music from the final song merrily playing in my mind:

> Then sings my soul,
> My Savior God to Thee,
> How great Thou art,
> How great Thou art!

Chapter 9

The New Age Center Converts to "Christianity"

A couple of weeks after the Kenneth Copeland convention, Muriel made a profound announcement during the midweek Bible-study class.

"Jesus has told me that the masters of the Hierarchy are no longer to be involved in the activities of the Lighted Way," she said. "We are now connected only with Jesus of Nazareth, the Father, and the Holy Spirit. I have been clearly informed that we are not to study any teachings other than the Bible."

We had been working with the masters for years, and I was not able to comprehend Muriel's radical statement. Finally, I rationalized that, since we had been studying the Bible for several weeks, perhaps the spirit supervision of our metaphysical center really was now coming directly from Master Jesus, and he was making appropriate changes.

I remembered reading in the Alice Bailey books that the supervision of a group is often transferred from one master to another. This transfer is supposedly part of the process known as the divine movement of energies. It seemed reasonable that if we were now supervised by Master Jesus, we would focus on the Bible and temporarily discontinue our work with the other masters.

A week passed since Muriel's interesting announcement. The night before the next study class was to be held, I awakened from my sleep. While in a state of semisleep, I received a clear, strange message. "You need to adopt a conventional religion," the inner voice said. Deeply impressed, I mentally took note of the message before falling asleep again.

When I awakened in the morning, the message was still in the forefront of my mind. Though I wrote it down in my journal, I had no idea what was referred to by the term "conventional religion."

Later that day, I attended the Bible-study class. Only a handful of people turned up, and we seated ourselves in a small circle. Muriel began her talk. "Last night Jesus awakened me and told me that Djwhal Khul is not one of us," she said abruptly. I leaned forward to listen carefully to what she was saying about my master.

"Jesus explained to me that Djwhal Khul's teachings are inaccurate. He is not a perfect being. Djwhal Khul cannot be involved in the Lighted Way now that we are following Jesus Christ."

I wondered what on earth Muriel was getting at. Looking over at my friend Peter, I watched for his reaction. His eyes flashed over at me, gave me a blank stare, and then focused back on Muriel. He looked as surprised as I felt.

"Jesus told me that Djwhal Khul has fallen," she continued. "He desired knowledge and became filled with pride. This caused him to consider himself more intelligent than he really was. He was totally mistaken in the statements he made in the Bailey books regarding the identity of Jesus."

I started to feel uncomfortable with what Muriel was saying. How could she put down my beloved master? I sat in stunned silence as Muriel explained. "Jesus of Nazareth was not of human descent as Djwhal Khul claims. He is a divine being. He is the only begotten Son of God. He was divinity incarnated in human flesh. He is God. Jesus is not a master who has had past lives. Djwhal Khul was wrong. Jesus is the Christ. He has more power than any master."

Then Muriel grinned and said, "I think Djwhal Khul may be Satan."

I was dumbfounded.

My anger welling, I almost got up to storm out of the class in protest over this blasphemy against my beloved Djwhal Khul and his teachings.

But I calmed myself and tried to sit tight and hear out the rest of Muriel's revelation.

She continued, "In the Bible, Jesus said, 'I am the way and the truth and the life. No one comes to the Father except through me.' It is absolutely true; there is no other way to reach eternal life than through Jesus Christ. You cannot obtain immortality through a master. A master or a guru can raise your consciousness, but at some point everyone has to come to Jesus. It is only through him that a person can receive eternal life."

I was now in a state of utter shock. It was the only time in six years of attendance at the Lighted Way that I had felt like walking out of the group. It was like torture listening to Muriel's preposterous statements. I felt relieved when the class was finally over, and I left immediately.

Feeling angry and confused as I drove home, I then recalled the message I had received in the middle of the previous night. The mysterious inner voice had told me I needed to adopt a conventional religion. I wondered whether this was the voice of the Holy Spirit telling me that I needed to become a Christian. I did not know what to believe; I certainly didn't accept Muriel's testimony at face value. My main question was, Is it really possible that the conventional Christian churches teach the truth about Jesus?

In a mood of utter suspicion, I attended the following week's Bible-study group. I wondered what incredible statements Muriel would make this time.

She began with another shocker. "Jesus has been explaining lots of things to me. During each night, he has been waking me from sleep and has been telling me the truth about himself and the plan of salvation. He tells me to write things down before I forget them, so I scribble messages on a note pad as he talks to me."

Muriel looked perfectly relaxed as she continued her dissertation. "Jesus told me that he has intervened in the Lighted Way to bring me into eternal life and to enable me to bring the knowledge of eternal life to others. He told me I was being influenced by satanic entities and was in danger of being led astray by false doctrines and half-truths. Jesus is now teaching me about the resurrection."

I felt insecure and intimidated as my total philosophy came under attack from the fundamentally new concepts Muriel expounded.

"Jesus has told me that the Lighted Way is now no longer a metaphysical center," she stated. "We are to reorganize ourselves as a Christian church. We will have to change our name."

I felt as if my whole belief system had been pulled from under my feet.

"We are going to do a lot of hymn singing," she continued. "We are going to do a lot of prayer work and Bible study. We are definitely not going to study any of Djwhal Khul's teachings." Muriel picked up her Bible and read several passages. We then had a prayer session followed by silent meditation and closed the meeting by repeating the Lord's Prayer.

I drove straight home. Confusion again clouded my mind. Walking into my apartment, I sank to my knees before the altar and prayed as sincerely as I knew how: "Heavenly Father, I ask you to bless me with wisdom and clarity of mind so that I may know the truth regarding these matters. I beg that the Lighted Way be protected from any false and astral influences. May only truth prevail. Heavenly Father, I ask these things in the name of our Lord Jesus Christ. Amen."

In my meditations, the voice of conscience gave me firm advice that I should not leave the Lighted Way, but should continue to attend the classes, even though I was unsettled over the changes taking place there. I still felt a deep love for Djwhal Khul and was reluctant to let go of the relationship with him. How could he be satanic? I wondered.

Gradually, I began to reason that perhaps Jesus really was the only begotten Son of God and was now calling me into his fold. One thought predominated. It was Muriel who had led me to the religious path in the first place. She obviously knew a lot more than I did about divine matters, and I needed to give her statements very serious consideration.

At the next class, Muriel again narrated what she had been told by "Jesus" during the previous week. She emphasized that only one path led to eternal life, the Christian path. "Ultimately all the people following the Hindu teachings will have to accept Christianity in order to be saved and obtain eternal life," she affirmed.

She stressed that to obtain salvation, one must believe in Jesus Christ, be his disciple, and become one of the "saints" described in the book of Revelation.

Muriel told us that the esoteric books were impure and misleading, and advised us to be on our guard against deceptive astral spirits who were trying to lead people astray. "These entities, or demons, may try to influence you and draw you away from the Christian path," she warned.

Picking up her large Bible, she began to read. "Put on the full armor of God so that you can take your stand against the devil's schemes. For our struggle is not against flesh and blood, but against the rulers, against the authorities, against the powers of this dark world and against the spiritual forces of evil in the heavenly realms."

She explained that this passage from Paul's letter to the Ephesians warns us about the evil powers and principalities lurking in the spirit realms. We need to go to Jesus in prayer and ask him for guidance and protection from satanic forces.

This idea of "satanic" forces intrigued me. It was a concept that Djwhal Khul had repudiated, not that Djwhal Khul's statements were supposed to matter anymore. According to Muriel's dissertation the previous week, she thought he might be Satan. I wondered whether Muriel really believed Satan existed.

My attention switched back to her dialogue. "Jesus of Nazareth is the Christ," she declared. "He is God. Of his own free will he decided to incarnate as a human being in order to take upon himself the karma, or sin, of the world and give humanity the opportunity of obtaining eternal life. Through his death on the cross, he lifted the karma of humanity. If we accept Jesus as our saviour, our personal karma is lifted from us; he takes over our lives and leads us into immortality."

I had never heard Muriel speak so powerfully. Her words struck deep into my psyche. It sounded as if Christianity were the religion closest to God, after all.

Raising my hand, I asked, "Muriel, do you think that there is a real being of supreme evil, called Satan?"

"I am not sure," she replied. "Jesus has talked to me only about satanic forces. There may have been a great devil called Satan. In the Bible, Jesus said, 'If you are not with me you are against me.' Everyone who is not a Christian is Satanic, in a way."

I didn't want to pursue the question further, so I remained silent. We had an intercessory prayer session and again closed with the Lord's Prayer.

During the following week I did a lot of soul-searching. Through Bible reading, prayer, and earnest meditation, I started to accept the idea that Jesus really was not of human origin and evolution, as Djwhal Khul had claimed. Concluding that Jesus was rightly the King of kings and Lord of lords, I decided to let go of all attachment to the masters and accept Jesus as my personal saviour.

Getting down on my knees in prayer, I humbled myself and cried out to God: "Dear Heavenly Father, thank you for sending your Son to die for our sins. Thank you for bringing me into this new light. I give thanks that I am saved by my belief in Jesus. I give you thanks for the gift of eternal life through the death of Christ on the cross. Thank you for his mission so that I can be forgiven of my sins and have my karma lifted. I ask for wisdom to understand your plan of salvation. I ask this in the name of our Lord Jesus Christ. Amen."

At this time, the Lighted Way was temporarily operated from Muriel's home, and we were not conducting any Sunday morning services. Muriel advised us to go to a Christian church each Sunday to worship the Lord. She stated that "Jesus" had instructed her to attend a particular church in her neighborhood. However, we could go to any church we were impressed to attend.

In response to Muriel's advice, I attended services at a variety of denominations in my neighborhood. The sermons were not as fascinating as Muriel's talks, but I enjoyed the opportunity of worshiping the Lord.

In response to directions coming from "Jesus," Muriel reorganized the Lighted Way as a Christian church group, choosing the name the New Lighted Way. We were to start as a house church prior to leasing a new center in a commercial building. Our brochures were embellished with the motto Jesus Is Lord.

My diary records the first Sunday morning service, held in early January.

We were just a small group gathered in Muriel's large apartment, sitting on neatly arranged folding chairs. The service started with the singing of a few contemporary Christian songs followed by a traditional hymn. Muriel prayed and asked for a blessing upon the work of the New Lighted Way. Ending the prayer, she invoked, "May all that we do glorify the Son. We ask these things in the name of Jesus Christ."

After we were seated, she read from the Gospel of John. "In reply Jesus declared, 'I tell you the truth, unless a man is born again, he cannot see the kingdom of God. . . . I tell you the truth, unless a man is born of water and the Spirit, he cannot enter the kingdom of God.' "

Muriel followed the scripture reading with a sermon based on the necessity of becoming a born-again Christian. She stated that at some time in the future, when she had access to a swimming pool, we could receive a water baptism from her. "For now, we have to be born again by accepting Jesus as our saviour," she declared.

After the sermon, Muriel conducted a candlelighting ritual. It was similar to the candlelighting ceremony we had been performing for years when we operated as a metaphysical church.

In turn, each person went up to the altar at the front. He lighted a candle from a source candle called the Christ candle, which was burning in the center of the altar table, and placed it adjacent to the Christ candle.

Muriel asked each person to kneel down before the altar. She laid her hands on their heads and recited a prayer of blessing. She then proceeded to channel a message from "God" for that person.

From Muriel's wording, it appeared that the Christ candle was now regarded as a representation of Jesus Christ himself, rather than being a vague symbol for the "Christ energy," a term used when we were a metaphysical church.

When it was my turn to go to the altar, Muriel told me to kneel down and hold my hands together in prayer. "Are you in need of any kind of healing?" she asked.

"Yes," I replied, "I have been having trouble with my gastric system again."

Muriel placed her hands upon my head and said, "Father in heaven, we ask for a healing of Will's stomach sensitivity. We ask that he will be completely healed from the tip of his toes to the top of his head. We ask this in the mighty name of Jesus Christ."

She now began to channel a personal message: "You are blessed by the Father. You will have oneness with him. You need to detach from all the metaphysical teachings, throw away all your books except for the Bible, and come into the personal presence of Jesus."

This message was difficult for me to accept. I had loved all my esoteric books. Returning home, I meditated on the advice.

The inner voice of conscience spoke to me. "Come unto me and I will give you rest. Seek ye first the kingdom, and all else shall be added unto you," it said.

Stepping out in faith, I decided to completely give myself to Jesus Christ. Throwing into the trash dumpster my library of metaphysical books, I cleaned out my whole apartment of all books, magazines, flyers, and brochures connected with the New Age. I resolved to spend my spare time meditating, praying, and reading God's Holy Bible. Regarding myself as a born-again Christian, I aspired to come into the living presence of Jesus as the sole means of my salvation.

This new focus did not mean that I gave up all my metaphysical beliefs. On the contrary, I still held to many of them. However, as I read the Bible, some of these beliefs started to come under pressure.

For example, I read a passage in which the writer of Hebrews makes a statement totally contradicting the doctrine of reincarnation. "Just as man is destined to die once, and after that to face judgment . . . " (Hebrews 9:27).

In my thinking, I attempted to make this statement compatible with my reincarnation beliefs by assuming the biblical writer was ignorant about the reality of past lives. He simply was not advanced enough in consciousness and knowledge at that time to know that man lived several incarnations.

Muriel herself was still talking about her own past lives. I concluded that if the reincarnation doctrine were inaccurate, then no doubt Jesus would soon inform us of our error.

My meditations encouraged me to live a sanctified life and withdraw from the secular world even more than I had while on the metaphysical path. I regarded my apartment as a kind of monastery with a population of one.

With candles and incense burning, I often knelt in front of the altar to pray, sometimes combining prayer with meditation as I remained on my knees for an hour or two. I still used the metaphysical visualization rituals and invocations, but modified them to be more in harmony with my new faith. My goal was to seek the living presence of Jesus Christ and obey the voice of the Holy Spirit.

"You are going to move into a new, closer relationship with Jesus," channeled Muriel one evening as I stood before her in front of the altar. We were conducting our candlelighting ordinance. Muriel's eyes were closed, and I assumed she was speaking in the power of the Holy Spirit.

"Tonight Jesus is going to wake you up out of your sleep and talk to you directly, just as he has been doing with me. He will give you a message of revelation. You will be surrounded with great glory, and you will walk in a cloak of glory."

I found the message interesting, but did not think about it again that evening. At the end of the service, I drove home, enjoying the Christian music playing on my car radio.

"This is an earthquake," I said to myself as I awakened in the middle of the night. A wave of fear swept over me.

My bed trembled.

I looked up, expecting to see the pictures swaying on their mountings. Strange, they were not moving.

Focusing my ears to listen for the creaking of the apartment-building timbers, I couldn't hear anything, even though my bed was still shaking. I thought, This is weird.

Suddenly, I heard a voice.

"Wilfred, I want you to take death seriously. You may not have long to live. I want you to exercise on a regular basis."

"Jesus," I exclaimed intuitively.

I carefully listened to hear whether the voice would tell me more. Everything was deathly quiet. I noticed my bed had stopped shaking. I felt strange, and a bit afraid.

Recalling Muriel's prophecy, I realized it must have been the voice of Jesus talking to me, just as Muriel had predicted earlier in the evening.

Lowering my head down on the pillow, I relaxed and took a deep breath. I thought, How unusual; he called me by my christened name, which I had not used for years.

"Jesus" seemed to speak to me audibly, but I heard it with some kind of "inner" ear. It was definitely quite different from the voice of my higher self, that clear voice of conscience which often spoke into my mind.

I felt concerned as I pondered on the content of the message. "Jesus" seemed to be warning me that my health was not very good. Maybe my cardiovascular system was in poor condition, and I lacked exercise. I concluded I had better do what "Jesus" advised and start exercising regularly, perhaps jogging.

Climbing out of bed, I wrote down the message. It had affected me profoundly. I was intrigued that "Jesus" had personally awakened me to give me a direct message. However, apprehension over the content of the message seemed to override my appreciation of this new level of experience with "Jesus."

I recalled how Muriel had often told us in the class that she had been awakened in the night by one of the masters, or recently, by "Jesus." She claimed she was then given prophetic messages. Now I understood what she had been talking about.

I wondered what was going to happen next in this new, close relationship with God.

As you are following my story at this point, it almost seems that the Holy Spirit was intervening in a miraculous manner at the Lighted Way to bring to us the true gospel. The "conversion" of our New Age center now becomes more suspicious. Let me describe to you what happened next.

At the following Bible-study group, Muriel began to speak. "Jesus has been teaching me many interesting things," she said as she opened her Bible. "I am going to read from First Corinthians, chapter fifteen."

She looked down and began to read. " 'So will it be with the resurrection of the dead. The body that is sown is perishable, it is raised imperishable; it is sown in dishonor, it is raised in glory; it is sown in weakness, it is raised in power; it is sown a natural body, it is raised a spiritual body.' 'For the perishable must clothe itself with the imperishable, and the mortal with immortality.' "

Muriel gave an explanation. "Through the power of Jesus Christ, one can start a process of translation into the resurrection body," she said. "The old self, the personality, has to be refined into the Christ self. It takes effort and discipline to do this, but Jesus gives us the strength and knowledge."

In my reading of the Bible, I had wondered how the resurrection fitted in with the New Age scheme of things. So I listened eagerly to Muriel's revelation.

"Through Christ's divine power, the actual atoms of the physical body are transformed into the refined atoms of the resurrection body. Once you have built up this body of immortality, you are able to live an eternal life here on the planet."

Hmmm, I thought, from what Muriel is saying, it seems that the resurrection is not going to be a rapture process, as most Christians assume.

She continued. "Only through the power of Jesus Christ can one end the cycle of death and rebirth, that process of reincarnation. If you go to Jesus, confess your sins, and ask him to transform your life according to his will, then your karma will be lifted. The power of Jesus will begin the process of building up the resurrection body of immortality. This is the spiritual body that the apostle Paul talked about. It is built out of the mortal body by means of the Christ energy coming from Jesus."

As I listened to Muriel, I recalled that for several years she had claimed that her body was undergoing a rejuvenation process. She had openly stated that she was gradually getting younger and would eventually reach an age of twenty-eight. She had asserted that once she reached this young age, she would live an immortal life here on the earth in the glorious New Age of love and light.

From what Muriel was saying, it sounded as if the Bible talked about the same process, but it was the resurrection power of Jesus that activated the transformation rather than some vague, cosmic "Christ energy."

Muriel again read from her Bible. "Blessed and holy are those who have part in the first resurrection. The second death has no power over them, but they will be priests of God and of Christ and will reign with him for a thousand years."

Looking up, she then explained. "This text from the book of Revelation describes the resurrection process I am going through. This process that translates the atoms of the mortal body into the refined atoms of the immortal body is known as the first resurrection. Those who translate through the power of Jesus are part of the first resurrection. They will live on this planet during the thousand-year millennium of peace and prosperity. This millennium is the New Age."

Muriel bent over and placed her Bible on the floor.

"The Bible teaches that there will be a second resurrection," she said. "It is for those who don't make it into the New Age. They fail to accept Jesus and thus do not undergo the translation. They will be judged and will get a second chance later."

Muriel paused and looked at us as if to invite questions. I didn't fully understand what she had said, but remained silent.

"Jesus told me that we are on the path of eternal Sonship," she continued. "We are to live a righteous life by following his example in the Bible. It is our goal to become sons of God and be one with the Father, just as Jesus was one with the Father."

Muriel beamed as she began to speak again. "Jesus informed me that I am now a member of the Melchizedek priesthood. It is the royal priesthood of Christ and is spoken of by the apostle Paul in Hebrews."

Everyone in the class sat motionless. I didn't know what to make of her statement. Who was I to contradict her status?

At the end of the lecture, Muriel invited the class members to come up to the altar to receive a blessing.

It is now clear that the Holy Spirit had not intervened at the Lighted Way. We were simply experiencing a deepening of the Mastermind's plot of deception. We were being deliberately converted into a counterfeit Christian church organization in order to attract a new type of clientele and fulfill a new mission. Our function was to help spread counterfeit Christianity.

Even though the Bible replaced all our former metaphysical textbooks and we called ourselves bornagain Christians, we still relied upon meditation as a means of receiving doctrinal information from "God."

IMPORTANT NOTE

To prevent any confusion, for the remainder of this book I will use *italics* to indicate that I am referring to the counterfeit version of the Godhead. For example, *Jesus Christ* and *the Father* will denote Satanic angels masquerading as Jesus Christ and the Voice of God, respectively. Where statements are made by others, the use of *italics* will indicate that in my opinion the counterfeit is involved, even though that person believed in all sincerity that he was dealing with the real Jesus or real Holy Spirit. *Italics* will also denote counterfeit divine qualities.

Chapter 10

The Melchizedek Priesthood

Standing in a bright and ornate palace, I appeared to have been taken up into the heavenly realms. Words cannot describe the beauty of the building's Roman-style interior. A wonderful atmosphere of peace and holiness pervaded the court.

Before me stood a beautiful woman with a shining, angelic glow on her face. Looking like some kind of divine priestess, she had a floral garland on her head and wore a long white gown. Her wonderful smile of joy was a delight to my beholding eyes.

In her hand she held a golden neck chain, from which hung a small brown wooden cross. It looked like a chain a priest might wear. The angelic being placed the chain around my neck, the wooden cross proudly hanging in front of my chest.

Her beautiful blue eyes were as deep as heaven itself. She smiled and said, "Well done, thou good and faithful servant."

I intuitively realized that I had just been initiated into the priesthood of *Christ*.

Suddenly, I awoke and found myself lying in bed. The dream was so lucid and powerful that I was convinced I had been taken up into the heavenly realms in my soul body and had undergone initiation into the priesthood.

I was impressed to purchase a real cross and chain as a token of my ordination. At a local Christian bookstore, I selected a wooden cross and chain that were identical to the ones I saw in the dream.

When I returned home, I lighted the two candles on my altar and burned incense. Holding a private devotional, prayer, and meditation service, I consecrated the cross and chain, solemnly placing it around my neck.

I regarded myself as having been called by God for training into the Christian priesthood and wanted to become a minister. It was my deepest desire to help save people from the illusions and glamours of materialistic living and bring them into eternal life through the consciousness of the grace given by *Jesus Christ.*

The next day, I attended the Sunday morning church service at the New Lighted Way. I was wearing my newly consecrated wooden cross hidden beneath my vest because I didn't want to be pretentious and have the cross visibly displayed. I regarded my selection for the priesthood as a sacred, private affair between me and God.

At my turn during our customary candlelighting ordinance, I walked up to the altar, lighted a white candle, and placed it next to the *Christ* candle. Muriel closed her eyes to channel a personal message for me from the *Holy Spirit.*

"I see you wearing a wooden cross suspended on a gold chain," she said. "Upon the spirit planes you have received an initiation into the priesthood. The *Father* is very pleased that you have accepted the offer of becoming a servant of *Jesus Christ.*"

Wow, I thought, it really did happen. My cross and chain are completely hidden from view, so the *Spirit* must have revealed one scene of my initiation to her.

Muriel continued. "You will be greatly blessed and rewarded for your decision to become a disciple of *Christ.* A glorious future is awaiting. You will eventually leave your current employment and be involved in evangelism."

Smiling with satisfaction, I returned to my seat.

Muriel had previously stated that she was a member of the Melchizedek priesthood. I thus assumed I had been initiated into this same priesthood also, although I regarded my status to be probationary until undergoing further training.

In remembrance of the death of my saviour and master, I resolved to wear the wooden cross at all times. I wanted it to be a constant reminder of my commitment to the sacred life of the priesthood.

Muriel began her sermon and talked about the necessity of living a pure life by following the example of Jesus Christ, as described in the Bible. She emphasized the requirement to obey the will of *the Father* as manifested through the voice of the *Holy Spirit*, but warned about the existence of satanic entities in the spirit realms that might try to lead one astray.

"One has to be very discerning," she advised. "If you are not sure whether a spirit entity is from *Christ* or is satanic, ask the entity, 'Are you of Jesus Christ?' If the entity is not from *Christ*, it will flee from you. The name of Jesus is the most powerful name in the universe. You can use it to protect yourselves from evil powers. For example, if you feel you are being oppressed by an evil force, you can use the invocation, 'In the name of Jesus Christ, I command that you leave.' The entity will have to depart."

After a pause, Muriel changed topics.

"Now, there may be a rapture. It is inferred in the book of Revelation. We will be part of the 144,000, the redeemed first fruits. I have not yet received full clarity on this from *Jesus*. But a time may come when all the saints are lifted up in the air and we can levitate. We will probably visit other planets."

My mind was starting to get confused again. I had thought I had the resurrection figured out; now this rapture idea had muddled things up. I concluded that I would have to meditate earnestly upon the matter and have faith that the *Holy Spirit* would reveal the meaning of the book of Revelation to me.

A couple of months passed. The annual Kenneth Copeland West Coast Believer's Voice of Victory Convention began at the Anaheim Convention Center. I was inspired to attend every evening during the week-long event. Copeland's topic for the convention concerned the covenant relationship existing between the Father and his people.

What a difference between my attitude at this convention and my attitude at the previous one. At the earlier convention, I had identified myself as a metaphysical New Ager, a disciple of the venerable Djwhal Khul. Regarding my master's esoteric knowledge to be far superior to the biblical knowledge of the Christians, I had gone to the convention merely as a spectator. I attended only because Muriel had praised Copeland so much and because the inner voice of my meditation told me to go.

Since that previous convention, much had changed. I now identified myself as a born-again Christian, even though I still felt part of the New Age movement. However, this did not make me feel any sense of separation from my Christian brothers at this visit as I lifted my arms in praise and glory toward God. I enthusiastically took part in all the singing. As we all joined hands, I prayed to the Lord Jesus, along with the 10,000-person congregation, and wholeheartedly pitched in my generous donations at the offering time.

When Brother Copeland preached, I eagerly listened to what he had to say, carefully following the Bible texts referred to. Regarding myself as one of the fellow believers, at the end of each evening I felt absolutely ecstatic after the final singing. I was filled with joy and felt high, as if I were walking on air. Rarely had I been so filled with happiness.

I even felt this joy while at work during the day. The songs of praise rang in my heart. For example, during one morning of the convention week, I was sitting at my desk at work when our company's outside salesman called me on the phone. He was a conservative elderly fellow whom I had known for several years.

"Will, how are you doing?" he asked.

I burst out in the most vibrant, enthusiastic, and happy voice imaginable, "I am doing absolutely fantastic!"

Our salesman was silent for a moment. Then he said in a serious tone, "Is there anything wrong?"

I assured him that nothing was wrong; on the contrary, everything seemed so very right.

At the end of each evening I returned to my apartment and on my knees gave thanks to *the Father* for bringing me into the full knowledge and power of *Jesus Christ*. The inner voice of meditation then encouraged me to attend the convention again the following evening.

Brother Copeland gave an altar call each evening for unbelievers to come forward and accept *Jesus Christ* as their personal saviour. I realized that I had already been born again, and it would not be appropriate for me to go down to the front with the new converts.

I wished Kenneth would have a special altar call for people who felt the calling of God to enter into the gospel ministry and were willing to publicly acknowledge that call. In honor of my ordination into the *Christian* priesthood, I wanted to respond to such a call. Underneath my vest I proudly wore my sacred wooden cross.

Much to my delight, on Thursday evening Kenneth announced the altar call I had longed for. He specifically asked only those people who had made a serious and dedicated commitment to enter the ministry to come forward.

There was no hesitation on my part. I rushed down the flights of stairs and joined the group surrounding the platform at the front of the arena. Oh, how much I wanted to be an evangelist like Kenneth Copeland, if *the*

Lord would only anoint me with the power.

Copeland was joined at the lectern by other members of his ministerial staff. They prayed for our blessing and asked God that we be given the gifts of the Holy Spirit to carry out our gospel mission. At the time, I did not anticipate how soon my ministry would begin.

Shortly after the convention, I received a phone call from Muriel.

"*The Father* has told me to move to Texas," she said. "I am going to close everything down here in Los Angeles and start the New Lighted Way in Fort Worth."

Her statement shocked me. She had been operating the Lighted Way in Los Angeles for more than twenty years.

"It appears that Texas needs to be told all about mystical Christianity," she explained.

Having observed Muriel's obedience and dedication over the years, I knew she would pull up her roots and carry out the direction, even though she appeared to be in her sixties and had lived in southern California for most of her life. I wished her well and expressed confidence that *the Lord* would take care of all her needs.

The Call to Evangelize

"Go down to the mall and preach."

I heard the words clearly inside my mind as I was kneeling in front of the altar in my apartment. It was a Saturday morning, and I had just begun my meditation period.

I said to myself, "What? Go preach at the mall?"

Listening for more information, I heard nothing further. Shrugging my shoulders, I carried on with my silent introspection.

For several weeks I had been devoting my weekends to the study of J. Gordon Melton's *Encyclopedia of American Religions*. Continuing with this reading, I spent the rest of the day at the local city library. The history of the various Christian denominations intrigued me. Accounts of the work of such greats as the Wesley brothers, Finney, the Campbells, Moody, and others captivated my interest.

A week passed. I began my weekend morning meditation as usual. "Go and preach in the mall," the inner voice remarked.

"What do you mean, 'go and preach'?" I asked in my thinking, as if telepathically addressing the originator of the mysterious command.

There was no reply.

Something special about the voice this time struck a chord of fear inside me. It was the same inner voice of conscience I had so often heard before, But this time it was especially gentle and precise, with a strange power that drew my attention.

I started to imagine myself boldly preaching to a crowd of shoppers congregating outside the entrance to the local mall. They inquisitively listened to my proclamation of the imminent return of *Jesus Christ*.

Laughing at the fantasy, I thought: Who knows, maybe *the Lord* wants me to become another John Wesley; instead of preaching outdoors to coal miners, I will be preaching to shoppers outside of malls.

I dismissed the message as something mischievous coming from the astral realms. After all, who had ever heard of preaching at a shopping mall? The idea was absurd.

Continuing with the meditation for about an hour or so, I received no further inspiration and closed with a prayer requesting that I be made a clear and pure channel for *Jesus*.

Later that day, I had to go to the local mall to do some shopping. As I walked up the entryway, a fantasy suddenly flashed into my mind. I stopped and imagined myself preaching to passersby right where I was standing. An uncomfortable feeling filled my stomach, and my emotions sank as fear gripped me.

"Does *the Lord* really want me to start preaching down here?" I asked myself. "Oh, I hope not," I sighed as I took a deep breath.

"Excuse me," a woman exclaimed as she brushed past pushing a baby carriage, jolting me out of the daydream. I proceeded to the store.

The next morning was Sunday. I meditated as usual.

"I want you to go down to the mall to preach," the voice of conscience said firmly.

"What was that? What did you say?" was the inquiring reply spoken in my thinking, even though I clearly heard the instructions.

A strange sensation of warmth appeared in the upper-central area of my back. The sensation seemed to be located in the heart chakra region.

In my mind, I asked, "Is this some kind of joke, or is this a real direction coming from *God*?"

If it's from *God*, I thought, what exactly does "preach" mean? Am I supposed to go to the local mall and stand at the busy entrance, waving a Bible in my hand as I loudly preach to the people?

"No, no, this is just wild nonsense thinking," I reassured myself. "My mind is getting carried away; I need to discipline my thinking more carefully." I tuned in to the deeper levels of my higher self, trying to get clarification on the matter.

"Yes, I want you to start preaching to people at Del Amo shopping mall. It is now time for your ministry to begin," the inner voice stated.

I broke into a cold sweat. Closing my mind's openness to the cosmic, I brought the meditation to a prompt halt. I didn't want to listen to any more nonsense.

During the following week, I had several flashbacks to the fantasy of preaching to people at the mall. An uncomfortable uneasiness gripped me every time the idea came into my mind.

I reluctantly started to entertain the idea that maybe the *Holy Spirit* was speaking to me and really was asking me to go to the mall and preach the gospel. A morbid apprehension arose that would not go away. The command become an obsessive "thoughtform," a powerful and persistent idea that cried out for action.

My meditations now clarified exactly how I was supposed to preach to people. I was not being instructed to stand at the mall entryway and preach. Rather, I was to approach individual people in the mall and witness to them about *Jesus Christ.* I was to tell them about his soon coming appearance on the planet.

The inner voice informed me that this witnessing work was a form of preaching; it was preaching to individuals. The voice stressed that this personalized preaching was a valuable work in spreading the gospel, as well as being excellent training for future evangelizing work of a more exalted kind.

The idea of witnessing to strangers in the shopping mall petrified me. I resisted every command to do it. Each evening and weekend I came up with one excuse or another as to why I was not able to go to the local mall and witness to the lost souls.

Sometimes the excuse was, "I am not ready for it yet"; sometimes it was, "I am not in the mood." At other times I deliberately procrastinated in my secular duties so that I did not have time left in the evening to go to the mall.

In spite of loathing the witnessing idea, I believed that if *Jesus* were asking me to do it, then somehow I had to be courageous and do the work, irrespective of how much I dreaded it.

A few days later the inner voice of meditation once again told me to witness at the local mall. Again, fear gripped me. I had been hoping *the Lord* had forgotten all about this witnessing work.

I came up with several excuses why I could not go witnessing that evening: I was too tired; I didn't feel like it; I would not be successful anyway; I would go tomorrow instead.

Tomorrow came. I felt awful all day at work. The

prospect of witnessing after work depressed me terribly, and I felt sick with worry. It seemed like the stimulation to do witnessing work had completely taken over my life. I thought about it constantly and was powerless to stop the obsession.

"You have to do my work," the voice of *Jesus* exhorted throughout the day.

I frequently looked at my watch in dread of quitting time.

Finally the dreaded hour arrived.

"I am not going to do it," I said to myself. I copped out, consoling myself with the thought: Tomorrow I will feel different about it; the worry and anxiety have made me feel too fatigued to do anything this evening.

I decided to rest up and go to bed a little earlier than normal. Burying myself in the blankets, I welcomed sleep.

I woke up at around one o'clock in the morning, feeling absolutely terrible. The fact that I had not obeyed the order to witness in the mall seemed to haunt me.

The inner voice of conscience taunted me. "You must do my work," it asserted. "There is no escape. You have aspired to take up your cross and follow me. Why don't you do it?"

Tossing and turning, I tried to get back to sleep. But no sleep descended to take me out of the misery.

In my imagination I pictured people fishing in the darkness from the pier at Redondo Beach. I was aware that even at this time of night a handful of fishermen would be on the pier.

"Get up and witness to the fishermen right now!" the inner voice commanded.

"Get up," it blasted.

Wanting to hide, I pulled the bedcovers tightly around me.

As I lay in bed, I felt so depressed that I wanted to die. The oppressiveness was so powerful that I felt actual nausea; my stomach then convulsed involuntarily, and I had to sit up to suppress it. Rationalizing that *Christ* must have totally forsaken me, I concluded I was feeling the utter emptiness of life without *God.*

Recalling my frustrating experience of resisting the orders to use my credit cards to make thousand-dollar donations to support the Lighted Way, I remembered how futile my resistance was. I perceived only two choices were before me: Either I committed suicide, or I did exactly what *Jesus* was commanding. Unable to bear the terrible oppression any longer, I had to do something.

I finally reasoned that doing the unpleasant witnessing had to feel better than the way I was feeling, so I gave in and decided to go witnessing to the fishermen.

As soon as I started to get out of bed, I immediately felt better. I perceived that this scenario was in operation: if I obeyed *God*, I felt better; if I disobeyed him, I felt depressed as he withdrew his grace.

In the quiet of the night, as I slowly got dressed, a particular biblical text came into my mind. Jesus is making a statement to Peter:

> Feed my sheep. . . . When you were younger you dressed yourself and went where you wanted; but when you are old . . . someone else will dress you and lead you where you do not want to go (John 21:17, 18).

Having read the text a few days before, I now applied it to my situation. I thought: When I was younger I did as I pleased, living a rebellious and worldly life. Now that I am older, *God* is leading me to places where I do not want to go.

I concluded that there could be no turning back from my ministry. My choice was to obey *God* or face the deathly depression of separation from him.

Picking up my Bible, I left the apartment and drove toward the pier.

The Mastermind's demons had gained total control over my life. I had become a slave to their will. The fact that I carried a Bible and preached about *Jesus Christ* did not mean that I was a true witness for Christ, even though I looked like one.

Chapter 11

Preaching on the Boardwalk

"Earthquake!"

It was my first thought.

Fear and anxiety gripped me.

I had been suddenly awakened in the night. My bed trembled and shook.

Lifting my head up off the pillow, I looked up at the dimly lighted picture hanging on the wall opposite me. Strange, it was not moving back and forth as I had come to expect during an earthquake.

I listened for the sound of the building timbers creaking, but heard nothing.

A memory flashed into my mind: The last time this had happened was when *Jesus* awakened me to give me a special message.

With the bed still vibrating, a voice suddenly spoke into my ear.

"I am coming soon. You have got to do my work. Time is running out."

It's *Jesus*, I thought. The voice was unmistakable. It had a strange calmness overlaid with a tone of authority.

I strained myself to hear more.

There was only silence. I also noticed the bed had stopped shaking.

In my mind I had the powerful, intuitive thought that

137

Jesus was going to permanently appear in the world in about fifteen years' time. It was as if *Jesus* had implanted that knowledge directly into my brain, without my having consciously heard it.

The message from *Jesus* sent a wave of anxiety right through me. I knew I had been dragging my feet when told to do one-on-one personal witnessing to people in the shopping malls. I felt guilt about my timidity.

As I lay in motionless introspection, I realized that the purpose of *Jesus*' message was to inform me that I needed to make haste in my evangelizing efforts. Time was running out. I needed to make a greater effort to help proclaim the good news of his soon return so the world would be ready to receive him when he made his public, physical appearance, his glorious second coming.

In spite of my fear and reluctance to do the witnessing work, I resolved to put much more effort into my commitment to carry out the will of my master, no matter what he told me to do.

I thought about the prospect of *Jesus* returning at the turn of the century. What an incredible event that would be. I was sure I would receive my due reward from him when he came.

A couple of weeks passed. Early on a Sunday morning, I started my meditation as usual. After lighting candles on the altar in my apartment, I said intercessory prayers, concluding them with, "I ask this in the name of Jesus Christ."

After about a half hour of deep meditation, I started to receive clear directions from my inner voice of conscience. "Go down to Venice Beach and preach the gospel," it said.

Fear flooded over me. Though my entire body started to feel hot, I especially noticed a strong sensation of heat in the area of my heart chakra. I tore off my sweater, even though the room was fairly chilly. The energy present felt powerful.

I seemed to know intuitively that the direction was for

real because the energy was so strong. I fantasized preaching the gospel to a small crowd of curiosity seekers on the beach boardwalk.

I thought to myself: If *God* wants me to start preaching in public, I will have to do it. It seems I have received the commission. I don't want to go, but the time has come for me to start public preaching.

I reasoned that every disciple sooner or later receives the call to deny himself and take up his cross. Now it was my turn to die to self.

The inner voice spoke again: "The harvest is plentiful but the workers are few," it said quietly.

Then another Bible verse came into my mind as I contemplated the project before me: "Anyone who does not take his cross and follow me is not worthy of me. . . . Whoever loses his life for my sake will find it."

In my imagination, I again fantasized, seeing myself standing beside the beach boardwalk. I held a large Bible in my hand and boldly preached to the people passing by. The more I thought about the scene, the more I filled with apprehension. What if no one will listen? What if someone starts to become violent with me? What if someone calls the police?

I reasoned that if I were to become an evangelist, I would have to make a start somewhere. Who knew; perhaps I would build up as large a ministry as Kenneth Copeland's.

In a way, the idea of preaching the gospel at the busy beach boardwalk seemed a more acceptable proposition than doing one-on-one witnessing in the fashionable malls.

I decided to obey the meditation command without further hesitation. I knew it would be useless to resist anyway. I thought, If *God* wants me to preach, then that is what I will have to do. All preachers have to start sometime; perhaps it is better to be thrown straight into the deep end. I further reasoned that it appeared *God* wanted me to dispense with seminary training and all that sort of thing, and I was required to just get out there and preach the Word.

"Do it. Go," the inner voice kept prompting as I continued with my meditation. "The power of *God* will be with you. Go!"

Without further introspection, I said special prayers for blessing on my preaching effort. Then I walked over to the closet and pulled out my best brown suit. All the great preachers on TV seemed immaculately dressed in a suit, collar, and tie. I reasoned that I should dress the same way. I straightened the tie in the mirror, picked up my Bible, and headed toward the boardwalk in my white, late-model Pontiac Sunbird.

During the fifteen-mile drive to the beach, I soon started to feel absolutely sick in the pit of my stomach from fear. In spite of my resolve to do the will of my *Lord*, at every intersection, I felt like aborting the trip and driving away somewhere to escape. How nice it would be to visit a museum or hike in the mountains or just drive out into the desert.

My wandering imagination was brought to attention by the stern voice of my conscience. "Keep straight ahead," it scolded.

"Go to the beach and preach."

"You have to do this work."

"Time is running out."

"Go and preach."

I fantasized being ridiculed by teasing unbelievers. I imagined someone confronting me and threatening to call the police if I didn't stop disturbing the peace. I started to hope that the drive to Venice would never end, or that with luck, I would be involved in an accident.

However, no matter how sick with fear I felt inside, I was determined to respond to the great commission call. I had faith that I would receive divine protection. Perhaps even *Jesus* himself would stand beside me unseen and would assist me in my debut performance.

Feeling hot and uncomfortable in the car, I turned up the air conditioning to high. My chest tightened as if a thick steel band was squeezed around it.

"Keep going. Don't back down now," the voice interjected.

Finally I joined the queue at the parking lot entrance. In a state of shock, I observed the area. It had been some five years since I had last visited the boardwalk as a curiosity seeker, and I had forgotten what a dilapidated, run-down area it was.

I decided to first explore the mile-long main section of the boardwalk in search of a suitable location were I could stand and effectively preach to the passersby.

I walked down the busy, crowded fifteen-foot-wide pedestrian street. An assortment of mostly older buildings—housing cafes and stores—lined the inland side of the boardwalk. The ocean side of the boardwalk comprised a wide strip of grass-covered park area dotted with palm trees. Street vendors lined the sidewalk, selling all kinds of gadgets. At intervals, street performers peddled their artistry. I saw a fire eater, several solo musicians, musical bands, and even a chain-saw juggler.

The farther I walked, the more dejected I became. I brushed past hobos who looked mentally ill and in need of psychiatric care. Others suffered from horrible sores and skin diseases. I walked past punk rockers with large safety pins piercing their ears and with tattoos displayed on their arms. Homeless out-of-towners with sleeping bags strapped to their backs hobbled along, looking as if they were searching for their fortune.

While my attention seemed to focus mainly on the bums, they were actually in the minority. Regular weekenders taking a leisurely stroll in the sun made up most of the crowd. Some of the passersby even looked like affluent businessmen taking their wives out for an interesting Sunday adventure.

I had lost all enthusiasm, but forced myself to continue searching for a suitable preaching spot. The noise, the stench of booze, and the aroma of marijuana started to become sickening. I passed one street performer who appeared to be some kind of circus daredevil. He had spread out a large plastic mat covered with broken glass. His repertoire of feats included walking barefoot over broken glass bottles with sharp, jagged edges.

"I have had enough!" I said angrily to myself when I saw what he was doing. "This place is not for me."

In my thinking I said, I don't care what *God* wants me to do; I am not going to preach here."

Turning around, I headed back to the car in disgust, shocked to think that *Jesus* would send me to this terrible abode of evil. In a temper I told myself, The idea to preach at this place must have been a joke. I am never ever going to return.

Jumping into the car, I slammed the door and roared off.

The next Sunday morning during my meditation, I received an impression to attend a certain Christian church that I had never been to before but which I had passed each morning on my way to work. I had often thought about attending it just to see what kind of church it was but had never made any attempt to visit it.

Christ's Community Church was fairly small and seemed to have a conservative atmosphere. I arrived early enough to attend the Bible-study class held in the pastor's office. We read one of Paul's shorter epistles and followed this with a prayer session to seek the Lord's blessing upon the worship hour.

As the organist began playing the prelude, I entered the sanctuary and sat down quietly in a pew. Opening up the program bulletin, I glanced over the order of service. The closing prayer hit me in the eyes; I couldn't believe what I was seeing. There before me was printed The Great Invocation—the most important prayer of the New Age movement. The prayer was commonly seen in the Alice Bailey books, the metaphysical works published by the Lucifer Publishing Company, later renamed Lucis Press. Of course, New Agers consider Lucifer to have been a great king of Israel, not a fallen archangel.

I thought it wonderful that this New Age prayer was used in some Christian churches, but was surprised to find it used in what appeared to be a conservative church.

The order of worship and the sermon were just like what I had come to expect in any regular Christian church. I saw absolutely no indication that this church was in any way connected with the New Age, other than the fact that the New Age equivalent of the Lord's Prayer was being used for the benediction. I very much doubted whether any of the congregation knew where the prayer came from. I thought, *The Lord* must have inspired me to come to this church to let me know that his New Age energy really is beginning to manifest itself, even in the traditional churches.

It occurred to me that *Jesus* was showing me that if I faithfully carried out my evangelizing work, I, too, could have my own Christian church, similar to this one. I even wondered if *the Lord* was planning to have me join this community church in order to assist in the introduction of other New Age ideas into its teachings.

I joined the friendly church members in their fellowship luncheon, but did not mention anything about my doctrinal beliefs or New Age background.

In my meditations, *the Lord* impressed upon me the need to return to Venice to start a beach ministry. However, I was informed that the ministry was not meant to be conducted quite the way I had originally visualized. I was given a new perspective as to how I should do my "preaching."

In meditation, I visualized myself standing at the side of the boardwalk. Beside me stood a large sign displayed on an easel, the type used by artists to hold their canvas. The controversial message written on the sign was designed to attract attention. People stimulated by the sign and its message would then come over to me and ask me about my religious views. In this way I would be able to witness effectively to them. I was given clear instructions regarding the design of the poster display, including the appropriate wording.

I proceeded to purchase the easel and art materials, and then carefully made the sign. After finishing it, I thought to myself: *Jesus* is very smart to have impressed me in such a way; the idea for the sign is brilliant. I was very pleased with it.

The inner voice told me that initially I was not assigned to preach out loud to the passing crowds on the boardwalk. *Jesus* wanted me to attract people's attention with the special sign and then witness to them individually as they asked me questions. In this way I could spread the gospel and gain practice in the skill of persuasive speech, a necessary prerequisite to any future public evangelizing activity.

Even though the new assignment better suited my personality, I was still apprehensive about going to Venice again. I kept wondering what *Jesus* would want me to do next and found myself hoping that the weekend would never come.

Saturday morning did arrive. During my meditation I received confirmation that I needed to proceed to the beach as planned. "You do not have any choice," the voice insisted. "You have to do this work; it is your destiny plan. *The Father* will bless you. Go forth in strength and preach!"

This time I left my suit and tie in the closet. I had been impressed to dress casually in order to blend in with the beach scene.

I packed the sign and easel into the trunk of my car and set off for Venice. I again felt a nauseating apprehension and tightening chest, but tried to ignore them. I knew that if I wanted to continue in *God's* grace, I had to do this work.

I remembered the biblical account of Jonah and his flight from the task the Lord had given him—to go and preach in the city of Nineveh. I felt like running away, just as Jonah had.

"Lord, why me?" I asked in my thinking.

"Why not someone else?"

"Why does it have to be me?"

There was no answer in reply except the words, "You have got to do my work."

I finally arrived at the boardwalk parking lot. My plan was to quickly scout around for a suitable spot and then, without any hesitation, set up the display sign and carry out my work. I had committed myself that, come what may, I would stay for at least a full hour.

Even though it was not quite midday, the boardwalk was already fairly busy. I walked briskly down the boardwalk, trying to ignore all the bums and dopers, and intent on finding a suitable spot to set up the sign.

About a quarter of a mile down the boardwalk a voice inside my mind suddenly interjected, "Here!"

"This is it, right here. This is the place," it exclaimed.

I was standing in front of a small Jewish synagogue positioned right up against the edge of the boardwalk. The façade was painted white and had two large brown wooden doors at the front, one with a large star of David painted on it. The front wall had Hebrew words written on it along with an English sign displaying the name of the synagogue.

I noticed that the street vendors and performers seemed to have avoided this little stretch of the boardwalk, as if giving respect to the holy place of worship. Across from the synagogue was a nice place where I could conveniently put up the sign and face the walkway. With the synagogue opposite me, it was a perfect spot. The people would have only two things to catch their attention as they walked by: my sign or, directly across from me, the synagogue.

I thought to myself, If Jesus preached outside the

temple in Jerusalem, I don't see why I shouldn't preach outside of a synagogue in Venice.

Hurrying back to the car, I unloaded my sign and easel, recited a prayer for God's blessing, and then hobbled along with the bulky equipment under my arms, feeling terribly self-conscious. I almost wished I could hide the sign until I arrived at my destination.

I was relieved to find the space still vacant. With a certain amount of trepidation, I set up the easel, placed the large sign on it, and stood at attention next to my grand announcement.

The sign caused quite a stir with the crowd. Immediately a young couple stopped in their tracks as they passed in front of me.

"Where is he, then?" the man eagerly asked.

The unusual sign had grabbed their attention. In the center of the large poster was a colorful copy of the famous Warner Sallman painting of the face of Jesus Christ. Above the picture of Christ's face was written in large, bright-red letters:

IF YOU ARE WAITING FOR THIS MAN TO COME, YOU ARE WASTING YOUR TIME.

Below Sallman's picture of Christ was written:

BECAUSE I CAN TELL YOU WHERE HE IS!

I eagerly replied to the couple, "He has never left this planet. He is still here. But he does not exist in a flesh-and-blood body anymore. He let go of his flesh body after the ascension. He now exists in his spirit body and lives upon the spirit realms."

"How do you know?" the man asked dubiously.

"I know because I have seen him," I replied boldly. "He has appeared to me, he has given me healings, and I am a follower of his teachings."

The couple seemed interested.

"You see, *Jesus* has never left the planet," I explained. "He is still here. After his ascension, he did not travel to somewhere in outer space."

Pointing up to the sky, I said, "The heavenlies are not some place out there. The heavenlies are right here on this planet." I waved my arms in an arc, indicating our present environment. "The heavenlies are simply a different dimension of our normal existence. Heaven is not some place in the cosmos; it is located right on this planet."

I asked the couple, "Have you ever had a vivid, lucid dream so powerful that, upon waking, you were convinced you had been to a real place but you didn't know were it was?"

The woman nodded her head as if she related to what I was saying. Her boyfriend gave me a blank stare.

"In those kinds of dream experiences, you have not been just dreaming. You have actually visited real places in your soul body. You have been on a trip to the lowest levels of the spirit realms."

I explained further. "Now *Jesus* does not live on those lower levels; he exists upon higher levels of the spirit realm. But those spirit realms are right here on our planet—they are just in a different dimension." Pointing to the ground, I commented, "*Jesus* is still right here in this world. He has the power to pass from the spirit dimension into our material dimension at will."

The couple now started to look a little confused, so I raised my voice.

"*Jesus* has power. He has the power to heal you and help you in your life. He can speak to you through the practice of prayer and meditation. He is really right inside of you. All you need to do is meditate, and he will teach you how to live abundantly. He will heal you. He is *God*, he is omnipresent, he is everywhere, and he has the power to heal you and bring wisdom into your life."

The male companion started to look a little disinterested. I struggled to hold his attention. "The voice of *God* is right inside of you, if you will only take the time to meditate and listen to him," I said.

I hesitated for an instant to catch my breath. The man nudged his companion to move on.

My sign was attracting a lot of attention. Some people laughed when they saw it. Others looked more serious, and then glanced at me, as if to say, "Hmmm, I wonder who this guy is."

When my legs started to tremble with tension, I deliberately breathed deeply, a technique I had learned in bioenergetics training years before. This deep breathing brought on calm and strength.

Three young punk rockers approached me.

"Where is Jesus, then?" one of them asked.

"He is right inside of you," I replied as I pointed to the youth's chest.

One of the youths asked sincerely, "In what way can he help me?"

"*Jesus* has power," I replied. "He is *God*. He can transform your life if you let him. For instance, if he took over your life, you could become president of General Motors. There is no limit to what *God* can do in your life. But you must meditate and seek his presence first."

I gave the guys further encouragement before they left.

At one point an elderly man started telling me how he liked to read the Bible. Glancing aside, I noticed a police patrol car slowly working its way through the people as it came up the boardwalk.

Shifting my focus back to the man, I commented, "Reading the Bible is good, but it has its limitations. It does not tell you what God wants to communicate to you right now. The only way to know God's will for you right now is to meditate and listen to the voice of the Holy Spirit."

The police car came nearer.

Feeling uneasy, I glanced over to the synagogue.

The car reached my spot and stopped.

I wondered whether I was doing anything illegal. Perhaps the synagogue people had filed a complaint.

The officer poked his head out of the open window and asked, "Where is he, then?"

His colleague in the car peered at me with a grin on his face.

"He is right inside your patrol car," I replied with a big smile on my face as I pointed straight at their vehicle.

I explained my gospel message to the officer. He thanked me and proceeded with his patrol.

Many people approached me and asked, "Where is he?" Sometimes they stayed for quite a while listening to my discourse. At other times they began to walk away after my opening sentence. Some people were very serious in their questions; others looked for fun and entertainment.

One man told me that he was a backslidden believer. At the end of our conversation he said he was going to start attending church again because of my encouragement.

The main emphasis of my message was to tell the inquirer about the reality of *Jesus'* existence on the planet and to tell him about the importance of meditation as a method for gaining access to his great wisdom and healing power. If I could only persuade people to meditate, I knew that the voice of the higher self—that clear, quiet voice of the inner conscience—would do the rest in bringing the person onto a spiritual path. I hoped the seeker would find the New Age *Christian* path.

I stayed at the beach all afternoon, witnessing to all kinds of people—Christians, Hindus, atheists, agnostics, and New Agers. For each type of person, I was careful to tailor my basic message to be acceptable for their individual background. The witnessing turned out to be a successful venture.

As dusk began to descend, I started to pack up. I returned home feeling tired, but exhilarated. It was as if

I had broken through a block by doing the work I had been commanded to do. The release and the inner joy I regarded as a special reward from *God* for my successful accomplishment.

The wonderful feeling of joy and exhilaration lasted for a few days. I felt really high and even looked forward to visiting the beach again the next weekend.

The sign did its job beautifully, enabling me to witness to a lot of people. However, I now realized that I needed a handout for seekers and passersby.

In my meditations I received the inspiration to write a brochure called "The Search for Happiness." I listed my ministry under the name Light of the Way, a variation on The Lighted Way. I chose the name in honor of The Way, the first name given to the early church as recorded in Acts. In order to have a contact address printed on this publication, I obtained a post office box and subsequently had hundreds of the brochures printed.

I spent almost every Saturday and Sunday afternoon witnessing at the beach boardwalk. The great feeling of exhilaration that I felt after my first visit was never repeated again. It was simply a matter of doing *God's* work, a somewhat tiring work, but a work that I had been specifically commissioned to do. I met all kinds of people and started several friendships, with some people coming to see me each week on a regular basis.

I learned to be more careful when speaking to my "fellow" Christians; I didn't want them to have the wrong impression about my ministry. It was best to first ask each inquirer if he was a Christian. If the person answered Yes, I phrased my ideas so that they were more compatible with traditional Christian beliefs. If the person answered, "No, I am not a Christian," I knew I had much more liberty in the statements I could make to them.

For example, when addressing New Agers, I would openly tell them that I used to be a New Ager. I informed them that *Jesus Christ* had come into my life, and I had become a New Age *Christian.* I told New Agers I had discovered that *Jesus* has far more power than my former Hindu guru, and I explained to them that *Jesus Christ* was head of all gurus and masters.

"*Jesus Christ* is King of kings and Lord of lords," I would say. "All masters and gurus are subordinate to him, and you are better off going right to the source of all power. If you pray and meditate upon *Jesus Christ*, you will start to have miracles happening in your life. That is what happened to me."

I was impressed to write a second brochure. This one discussed Christian meditation and gave specific instructions on how to do the meditation techniques I had learned at the New Lighted Way. I gave out copies of it to the diligent seekers.

After I had spent several weeks on duty at the beach, a few individuals started to come to me on a regular basis for counsel regarding their personal problems, usually difficulties they were having in their relationships or in their religious experience. At the end of most counseling sessions, I would rest one hand on the brother's shoulder, hold my other arm in the air, and say aloud a prayer of intercession. I concluded each prayer with this invocation: "Heavenly Father, we ask this in the name of our Lord Jesus Christ. Amen." One man with a history of mental illness gave me his address and asked me to keep in touch with him. I was impressed to write him a long letter of encouragement.

I became acquainted with a woman who lived in an apartment on the boardwalk very near to my spot. She confided that a couple of years previously she had seen *Jesus* appear right on the stretch of beach near where I had the sign. She said, "As I was sitting on that bench over there, suddenly a bright and shining figure appeared standing on the sand about thirty yards away. I knew it was *Jesus.* I turned around to a lady who sat next to me and said to her, 'Look there, can you see him?' After a few moments, *Jesus* mysteriously disappeared."

Some people hung around for a long time, asking me all kinds of questions. One lawyer asked me what I thought of the second coming of Christ. I happily explained the nature of that very important event.

"*Jesus* has already appeared to people on the planet," I told him. "But this is not his full second coming. *Jesus Christ* will soon appear in our world in a real physical body, just like the one he had in Palestine."

The lawyer then asked, "When will Jesus come?"

"I expect him to appear in about fifteen years. At least that is what he told me a couple of months ago."

The man grimaced as if surprised by my answer.

"He will soon materialize himself in another flesh-and-blood physical body," I continued. "He will then appear in the world permanently in order to claim his rightful position as Lord of lords and King of kings. This will be his second coming. He will come to set up his kingdom. He will inaugurate the millennium, and we will have a thousand years of peace and prosperity. The biblical book of Revelation prophesies all this."

"Will he appear in the clouds?" the man asked.

"Let me make one point clear. Do not expect *Jesus* to appear in the clouds of the sky with all his angels. It is not going to happen that way. The Bible term *clouds* is symbolic of etheric 'substance.' "

Another person started to listen in.

"When Jesus returns, the atmosphere surrounding him will sometimes have a mistlike vaporous quality to it. This is what is meant in the Bible when it says he will appear in clouds."

My statement was in total contradiction to the clear description Christ gave of his second coming, as recorded in Matthew 24:27, 30, 31.

On a few occasions, a whole group of people gathered around me to hear what I was saying. When this happened, I raised my voice and boldly preached to them in exactly the manner I had planned on doing the very first time I came to the boardwalk in response to the command of *Jesus* telling me to preach the gospel.

A few individuals offered to help me in my work. I became friends with one young man in particular. A newly baptized Christian and a keyboard player in a Christian band, he was very interested in my mystical experiences. We had dinner together on a couple of occasions, and I gave him counseling and encouraged him to practice meditation.

While I found the beach ministry almost enjoyable in a sense, I still loathed doing the mall witnessing work. I avoided doing it whenever I could and only did it when I was absolutely forced to.

I was supposed to do the mall witnessing in the evenings after work as a supplement to the weekend beach ministry, but I had done very little of it compared to what I sensed *the Lord* wanted me to do. Instead of witnessing, I often copped out by intentionally working late at my job and then going straight home to read my Bible or study other Christian literature.

One Sunday morning I received clear instructions to go down to Venice Beach as usual. As I was leisurely driving down the freeway, the inner voice suddenly burst forth in my mind. "Turn around," it said. "There is a change of plan. You have to do mall witnessing today. Turn back and go to Carson Mall."

"Oh no!" I exclaimed. "Is this for real?"

Feeling apprehensive, I did not know what to make of this unexpected intrusion, especially since I hated the prospect of going to the mall. Reasoning that the voice could have been nonsense coming into my mind from the astral realms, I listened for more. Not hearing anything further, I continued to the beach, although I felt a little guilty.

As I drove along, I completely missed my freeway turn-off. Strange, I thought, I have never done that before.

I proceeded on with the intention of taking the next

turnoff. I missed that offramp too. It was as if my mind had gone blank. I began to wonder if these gross navigational errors were omens indicating that I should have turned around when I originally heard the unexpected instruction. I started to feel uncomfortable and wondered whether I should turn back and go to the mall, but I reasoned that it was too late—I was already near the beach.

I meditated in the beach parking lot. My higher self seemed to tell me to stay at the beach and set up my sign as usual, but the direction was not very clear. Not receiving any further directions, I decided to stay at the beach.

I did the work successfully and stayed at my post all afternoon. My good Christian friend from the musical band came to visit me. He shared with me his vision that at some point in the future we should set up a stage and preach the gospel to the beach people, using loudspeakers and a live Christian rock band.

"This is exactly what I have thought myself," I told him. Then I shared other ideas I had on how I planned to expand the ministry in general, such as renting a recording studio and making tapes for radio broadcasting with purchased air time.

Trying to convince people to turn to *Jesus Christ* was tiring work. Dusk finally arrived, and I set off for home feeling drained and ready for a good rest. During the drive back home, I noticed I was starting to feel rather depressed. By the time I arrived home, depression haunted me like an assassin. I felt terrible.

As I walked into my apartment, the inner voice abruptly pierced into my mind. "See, you should have turned around and gone to the mall as I instructed on the freeway."

I realized that I had made a mistake in ignoring the surprise instructions.

"You have to be prepared for my instructions at all times," the voice of conscience reprimanded. "You must do exactly what I tell you. I demand obedience."

I started to feel anger toward *Jesus* for his reprimand, especially since I was exhausted from the long day of doing his missionary work. I looked up at the Sallman painting of Jesus that was hanging on the wall. I could not understand why he should withdraw his grace and allow me to be punished with depression, just because I made an error of judgment.

Anger boiled up inside of me. I suddenly grabbed a sharp carving knife from the kitchen counter. In a fit of rage, I lurched toward the painting of Christ. Standing in front of the picture, I aggressively pointed the cold steel blade at Jesus.

"You bastard," I said angrily.

My jaw tried to clamp down on the words.

"You _____ bastard. I spend all day doing your work, and then you try to torment me like this."

Then I started to shout in a muzzled voice, "You bastard. I hate you."

Furiously, I waved the knife in front of Jesus. "I could kill you for doing this," I shouted aloud.

After a moment's hesitation, I turned around and took a couple of steps away from the picture. Turning around again to face the painting, I pressed the steel blade against my stomach and glared at Jesus.

"You're goin' to push me into doing this," I growled as the impulse to kill myself by hari-kari erupted in my emotions.

There was silence.

I turned away and put the weapon down, trying to control my anger before doing something stupid.

Bending down, I took off my shoes. Suddenly I seized one of the shoes and repeatedly banged it on the floor in a fit of uncontrolled rage. I imagined that I was hitting *Jesus* right in the face.

BANG!

BANG!

BANG!

"You bastard!" I shouted at the top of my voice.

"You swine!"

"I hate you!"

BANG!

BANG!

BANG!

I repeatedly smashed the shoe violently onto the floor with all my strength. It was as if I were exploding from all the weeks and months of pressure that I had been subjected to in order to be forced to do the mall and beach witnessing work.

The requirement to send more $1,000 checks to Muriel in Texas had further aggravated my exasperation.

BANG!

BANG!

BANG!

My arm started to hurt.

I paused to catch my breath.

Looking up at the picture of Christ again, new rage burst out of me.

BANG! I pounded the floor again.

BANG!

BANG!

"You _____ bastard!"

"Don't you dare do this to me!"

"I'll kill you for this."

BANG!

BANG!

"You bastard!"

"I hate you!"

Exhaustion overcame me, and I finally stopped. As I knelt there—panting like a mad horse, my hand numb from the pain of bashing into the hard floor—I started to realize that what I had been doing was terrible. Collapsing on the floor, I begged for forgiveness and mercy. Tears ran down my face as, sobbing, I prayed to *Jesus*. "*Lord*, please forgive me. I understand why you are disciplining me so strictly. I know I have to overcome my weakness and be fully obedient to your will. Please give me the strength to overcome."

I believed that *Jesus* loved me and was stern because it was for my good in the long term, and because the mission of spreading the gospel had to go forward with haste. I told *the Lord* that I was sorry for my loss of temper and outrageous blasphemy.

Strangely, as I begged for mercy, I somehow sensed that *Jesus* was not at all offended by my outburst. I intuitively felt that he was laughing at me. It was a strong impression, as if I could clearly hear his laughter inside my mind. I felt that I almost didn't need to ask for forgiveness.

I reasoned that because *Jesus* was *God*, he knew about my frustration and chronic anxiety over having to do the witnessing work, and he must have completely forgiven me, even before I begged him for it. He had not been surprised by the tantrum.

Getting up off the floor, I noticed I didn't feel any remorse over my blasphemous statements. The guilt had gone. Intellectually, I knew I should feel guilty, but I didn't.

Walking into the kitchen, I noticed the depression had lifted. I felt hungry and started to make supper.

You may be wondering if I ever had any doubts regarding the identity of the spirit that ruled my life—whether he was the true Jesus. The truth is, I never suspected I was a slave to demons masquerading as agents of light. My confidence in the New Age path and the spirit guides had been built up over many years. Once I had read the Alice Bailey books, I became a devoted "believer" in the New Age, its spirit guides, and its philosophies. I then became an easy candidate for total "possession." Almost nothing could shake my faith in what I believed and cause me to doubt the authenticity of my spirit guide. Even my dedicated Bible reading could not pierce through the web of deception because I was twisting the meaning of many texts in an attempt to harmonize them with my existing metaphysical beliefs.

Satan has incredible powers of deception. This is why cults are so enslaving. The victims have built up an almost impregnable wall of faith around themselves based upon their acceptance of contra-Biblical doctrines. Once a person is immersed in cults, it takes almost a miracle to rescue him from the powers of darkness masquerading as agents of light. Satan's power is incredibly strong. No wonder even the elect are at risk.

Jesus warned:

> Not everyone who says to me, "Lord, Lord," will enter the kingdom of heaven, but only he who does the will of my Father who is in heaven. Many will say to me on that day, "Lord, Lord, did we not prophesy in your name, and in your name . . . ?" Then I will tell them plainly, "I never knew you. Away from me, you evildoers!" (Matthew 7:21-23).

Just because a person has a Bible in his hand and is preaching a gospel in the *name* of Jesus does not mean that the person is automatically a Christian, a true witness for the gospel of Christ. As indicated in the scripture above, the person who has a true relationship with Christ is "he . . . who does the will of my Father who is in heaven" (verse 21).

The will of the Father is revealed in the Bible. If anyone is teaching contrary to the Word of God, he cannot have the light of Christ. The Bible says, "To the law and to the testimony: if they speak not according to this word, it is because there is no light in them" (Isaiah 8:22, KJV).

Christians need to protect themselves from false teachers and erroneous teachings by following the example of the noble Bereans, who "examined the Scriptures every day to see if what Paul said was true" (Acts 17:11).

Chapter 12

Encounter With the Holy Spirit

"The Lord is inviting you. He's calling on you now. He wants you to come forward and be baptized. Why don't you accept him?" the preacher pleaded as the choir sang melodiously in the background.

Should I go forward and be baptized at this time? I was sitting toward the back of the congregation during my first visit to this particular church. The sanctuary was full, with around 150 people present.

The pastor had preached boldly as he repeatedly warned the congregation of the consequences of sin. At the end of the sermon, a lively instrumental band began to play. When the preacher sang along with the band, exhorting the listeners toward greater righteousness, most of the congregation began to stand up.

The preacher then made his plea for the unsaved to step forward and have their sins washed away in baptism. The choir modulated to a higher key to increase the tension.

On most Sunday mornings I attended a Christian church service prior to engaging in my ministry at the Venice Beach boardwalk. I usually attended a different denomination each week in order to educate myself regarding their various worship styles and beliefs. In my morning meditation I sometimes received specific instructions telling me to attend a certain congregation.

159

On this particular morning, I was directed to go to the Peace Apostolic Christian Church, located in the Los Angeles suburb of Inglewood. Not expecting anything special to happen to me at this church, I was destined for a big surprise.

I had originally been invited to this church by Dan, one of its members. Dan and I met one evening the previous week during witnessing work for *the Lord* in a local shopping mall. At the end of our interesting conversation, Dan invited me to his church.

Invitation to Repent of My Sins

The preacher continued his rousing baptismal invitation. "Jesus is speaking to your heart right now," he declared. "He is beckoning you to commit yourself to him."

I wondered whether I should step forward and be baptized. I recalled Muriel stating that at some point in the future she would conduct a baptismal service for the members of the New Lighted Way. I rationalized that it would be best to wait until I met up with Muriel again and was personally baptized by her.

"There is someone else here who has not publicly confessed his faith," the minister exhorted. "The Lord is calling on you to wash your sins away. Come forward and accept his forgiveness." The choir sang even more intensely.

"Perhaps I should do it now," I said to myself. "No, not yet; this isn't the right place," I countered.

Deciding to meditate on the matter, I closed my eyes and tuned inward. Immediately I had a flash vision of a being like Jesus Christ standing in front of me. He was dressed in a long white robe and held out his arms. "Come unto me," he beckoned.

I heard my mind confirm, "The time is now. Get baptized!"

My stomach turned queasy. The palms of my hands began to perspire.

But without further hesitation, I jumped to my feet and walked nervously to the front.

The entire congregation cheered and shouted. "Hallelujah!" "Praise the Lord!" "Hallelujah!"

As I was led into a changing room, my guts sank into a nervous quiver. A deacon handed me a white baptismal robe. My initial anxiety seemed to melt away as I put on the garment. In its place, excitement blossomed at the prospect of being baptized.

The deacon led me to the baptistry at the very front of the sanctuary. Stepping down a ladder, I eased into the icy water.

"Will Baron, do you repent of your sins and accept the Lord Jesus Christ as your personal saviour?" the pastor asked.

"I do," I replied, nodding my head.

It was not easy for me to listen to the words of the preacher standing next to me in the water. Ever since I had left the changing room, the inner voice of *Jesus* had been talking to me with power.

"There is a change of plan," the voice announced. "Do not go to Venice Beach this afternoon. Instead, witness to the people at Carson Mall."

The pastor raised his arm in the air.

"I baptize you in the name of Jesus Christ for the remission of your sins."

"You have to do my work," *Jesus* scolded.

I felt myself being pulled backward. Cascading water flushed over my head.

The voice of *Jesus* was relentless. "By being baptized, you are now totally committing yourself to do my work," it emphasized sternly. "There is to be no more hesitating, complaining, or procrastinating."

I stumbled up the ladder out of the baptismal tank.

"Go forth and minister with greater zeal," *Jesus* commanded.

As I walked from the baptistry, members of the church staff approached me. "Praise the Lord, Brother

Will," they congratulated as they shook my hand. "Hallelujah!" "Praise the Lord."

Jesus continued his strict instructions: "You are now to spend all of your spare time working for me," he commanded. "Go down to the mall and witness to those poor lost souls. Tell them about my soon return and the glorious kingdom I will set up on this planet."

In dripping attire, I was escorted back to the changing room. After toweling and putting on my clothes, I left the room and began walking down the corridor. An elderly, heavyset woman approached me.

"Now that you have been baptized, would you like to receive the gift of the Holy Spirit?" she asked in a gentle voice.

I sensed that she must be some kind of church elder. "Holy Spirit?" I responded, with a questioning frown.

"Yes. Now that you have been baptized of water, you can be baptized of the Holy Ghost, if you ask for it," she declared. "But you must want to receive it."

"You mean I can receive the Holy Spirit right now? Here?" I inquired doubtfully.

"Yes, this is what the Bible promises. Everyone at Peace Apostolic who has been baptized and who then asks for the gift of the Holy Ghost has received the baptism of the Holy Ghost, as evidenced by the speaking in tongues."

After a pause to catch her breath, the woman repeated her question. "Do you want to receive the Holy Ghost?"

I focused inward to listen to my higher self. "Do it," I clearly heard.

"Yes, I'd like to receive the Holy Ghost," I told the woman.

She led me into what appeared to be the church committee room, where I took a seat at a large polished wooden table. Telling me she would return shortly, the woman walked out of the room.

My mind drifted back to when I first met Dan in the

mall a few days before. At the time, I was doing my mall witnessing activity in the evening after work. When I first approached Dan, he was sitting alone on a bench. I initially asked him if he were a Christian.

"Oh yes, I am a Christian. I am a born-again believer, and I have received the baptism of the Holy Spirit."

"Baptism of the Holy Spirit? What is that?" I asked in surprise. "Do you mind if I talk to you about it?"

"No, I don't mind at all. I'll be glad to tell you about it. Sit down," he invited.

"My name is Dan," he said, introducing himself. He proceeded to tell me how he accepted of the Lord and how he later received the baptism the Holy Spirit. He carefully explained that receiving the gift of tongues was not the same thing as receiving the baptism of the Holy Spirit. He stressed that the gift of tongues was only an outward manifestation of the gifts of the Spirit.

"Speaking in tongues is not the thing to desire," Dan emphasized. "The thing to desire is the baptism of the Holy Spirit."

Finding the topic interesting, I bombarded him with questions.

"You know, Will, when you have been baptized by the Holy Spirit, unusual things can happen as the spirit works through you. For example, it is not by accident that we have met one another. The Holy Spirit brought us together."

"Oh yes, I can appreciate that," I responded.

Dan continued, "Five minutes ago I was walking out of this mall, right out of that exit." He pointed to a near-by exit. "All of a sudden an inner voice told me to turn around and sit on one of the benches."

I thought, Inner voice, hmm, that's interesting.

"I couldn't understand why I should go back and sit down," Dan commented. "But I could sense the Spirit prompting me. So I came over to sit on this very bench. Just a few seconds after I sat down, you walked up to me."

I was fascinated. I hadn't realized that regular Christians received instructions from inner voices just as I did.

"It was the Holy Spirit," Dan affirmed. "He was telling me to sit on this bench, because the Holy Spirit wanted us to meet. We did not meet by chance; it was by divine intention. The Holy Spirit works in mysterious ways."

Deeply intrigued by Dan's claim to have been baptized by the Holy Spirit, I asked, "Dan, tell me. How can I receive the baptism of the Holy Spirit?"

He looked me straight in the eye and said seriously, "You need to attend a church that has the Holy Spirit and believes in the baptism of the Holy Spirit. You won't receive the gift of the Holy Spirit while among people who don't believe in it."

Dan invited me to his church and left me with directions on how to get there.

My attention suddenly returned to the committee room at Peace Apostolic. The church elder had reentered the room, accompanied by a younger woman, who proceeded to sit down at the opposite side of the table. Apparently, this younger woman had just been baptized, and the two of us appeared to be the candidates for receiving the gift of the Holy Spirit.

The church elder seated herself at the head of the table and handed each of us a King James Version Bible. Picking up her own Bible, she started to leaf through its pages.

I thought to myself, I have had so many mystical experiences as a devoted New Age Christian that I am sure *God* will consider me a suitable candidate to receive the special gift of his Holy Spirit.

The church elder began to speak.

"The Bible tells us that if we repent and are baptized, we will receive the gift of the Holy Ghost. This is promised in Acts chapter two, verses thirty-eight and thirty-nine."

She looked down at her Bible, adjusted the positioning of her round-lensed spectacles, and read the two verses aloud. "Peter said unto them, Repent, and be baptized every one of you in the name of Jesus Christ for the remission of sins, and ye shall receive the gift of the Holy Ghost. For the promise is unto you, and to your children, and to all that are afar off, even as many as the Lord our God shall call" (KJV).

She looked up at the young woman and me. "The Bible promises the gift of the Holy Ghost to those who repent and have been baptized. You have repented and are baptized. Shortly you will receive the gift of the Holy Spirit. Everyone at Peace Apostolic who has been baptized and who wants the gift of the Holy Ghost has received it. We have never had anyone who has not received the gift."

With that kind of guarantee, I started to anticipate something marvelous happening.

The elderly lady continued to explain, "The Bible tells us clearly that the evidence of receiving the Holy Ghost is the ability to speak in tongues." She then read Acts 2:4 and Acts 10:44-46.

My thoughts wondered back to the conversation with Dan in the mall. I recalled his telling me that few Christians had received the baptism of the Holy Spirit and that the gift was important.

The church elder quoted a couple more texts related to the Holy Ghost and the speaking of tongues before asking us whether we believed what we had just read. When we replied Yes, she stood up and asked us to follow her into the sanctuary. It was deserted except for a small group of young women standing near the front, who were identified as assisting ministers.

The two of us were asked to kneel at the altar rail. The young women surrounded us.

"In order to receive the gift of the Holy Ghost," the elder instructed, "you have to thank Jesus for saving you. Say out loud, 'Thank you, Jesus.' Keep saying it until the Holy Ghost comes upon you."

Closing my eyes, I folded my hands and quietly said,

"Thank you, Jesus, for saving me."

"Louder. And keep saying it," the elder encouraged.

"Thank you, Jesus, for saving me. Thank you, Jesus, for saving me," I repeated.

"Don't stop," interjected one of the young assisting ministers. "Keep repeating, 'Thank you, Jesus.' 'Thank you, Jesus.'"

"Thank you, Jesus. Thank you, Jesus," I cried out.

"Thank you, Jesus. Thank you, Jesus."

"Thank you, Jesus. Thank you, Jesus."

"Thank you, Jesus. Thank you, Jesus."

I stalled to catch my breath.

"Don't stop!" another minister shouted. "Keep saying it. Aren't you glad Jesus has saved you? Keep thanking him for it."

I continued to repeat "Thank you, Jesus" several times over.

"Louder!" bellowed another assistant. "Shout at the top of your voice. Tell Jesus how thankful you are. Come on, keep saying it, 'Thank you, Jesus.' 'Thank you, Jesus.'"

The other candidate and I continued to repeat the phrases we were instructed to shout.

The young assistants began to act like cheerleaders, shouting encouragement and exhorting us to keep repeating "Thank you, Jesus."

Suddenly the crash of something falling interrupted us. My eyes glanced open. In the excitement, one of the assisting ministers had accidentally fallen back against the pulpit, almost knocking it over. In the commotion, the large wooden cross in front of the pulpit was knocked off and crashed down upon the floor.

Quickly closing my eyes, I resumed thanking Jesus for my deliverance from damnation. The cheerleaders continued their exhortations as the sanctuary echoed with the din of our plea.

After what seemed like ages, my voice became hoarse with fatigue. How can this be a "gift" from God if I must work so hard for it? I wondered.

Immediately I countered this negative thought with a positive one: While I am here, I should do everything I can to obey the instructions; I should give it everything I've got.

"Thank you, Jesus," I immediately shouted in earnest, repeating it several times.

I recalled the statement made by the church elder that every candidate at Peace Apostolic had received the baptism of the Holy Spirit. I clung to the belief that if I kept doing as I was told, I would eventually receive the gift.

After several more minutes of chanting, I had difficulty speaking, as if my jaw were ready to go into some kind of spasm.

The elder and assistants became excited and implored, "Let the words come. Don't resist; just let them out."

I tried to speak, "Thank you, Jesus," but couldn't. My lips were quivering in an involuntary spasm.

The candidate next to me emitted a shrieking, babbling sound, a bit like Swiss yodeling.

"Keep going. Don't stop," an assistant blurted as I momentarily lost concentration listening to the other candidate.

Disciplining myself to continue until I received the gift, I noticed that the quivering of my throat soon changed into an utterance in a language I couldn't identify. Soon it became easy for me to speak out in this peculiar tongue. I felt as if I were channeling, just the way I used to do in the Lighted Way channeling groups—but this time I was channeling in an unknown language. I did not know what the words meant; the tongue sounded something like I imagined Russian to sound.

I was relieved when it was over, for I felt exhausted.

The sanctuary was silent. I opened my eyes. The assisting ministers were picking up the wooden cross and securing it back in place in front of the pulpit.

The elder was quietly kneeling beside me. I asked her whether she understood the language of the Holy Spirit.

"No," she calmly replied. Then she asked me gently, "What are you going to do now?"

Without hesitation, I boldly replied, "I am going to do *the Lord's* work. What else is there to do?"

I was referring to the mall witnessing task that the voice of *Jesus* had commanded me to carry out that afternoon. I got up and left.

As I write this book, I can't help but compare the experience at Peace Apostolic with a later baptism I received. This water-immersion ceremony occurred a few months after the real Holy Spirit had rescued me from the bondage of Satan and his evil web of deceit. On this latter occasion, I was baptized into a relationship with the authentic Jesus Christ, God and Son of the Father Most High.

As I entered the water, no voices hounded me to do their work. I spent the entire day filled with the simple joy of peace in the Lord. I was experiencing salvation by grace—salvation by faith in what Jesus had done for me.

Commentary on Satan and Gifts of the Spirit

When I spoke in tongues at Peace Apostolic Church, it was obvious that the manifestation could not have been the work of the Holy Spirit because I was a disciple of Satan. It also seems to me that the methodology used by the Peace Apostolic Church to precipitate the "gift" of the Holy Spirit is also nonscriptural. The repetitive shouting of "Thank you, Jesus" is contrary to the admonition of Jesus in Matthew 6:7: "When you pray, do not keep on babbling like pagans, for they think they will be heard because of their many words."

You may be wondering whether Satan has the power to counterfeit the gifts of the Holy Spirit—such as healing and speaking in tongues—in our day.

Jesus stated that "false prophets will appear and perform signs and miracles to deceive the elect" (Mark 13:22).

Think back to the days of the prophet Elijah. During the reign of King Ahab, God's prophet challenged 450 prophets of Baal to a contest on Mount Carmel to prove who was the true God, Baal or the Lord. Each contestant built a stone altar with wood and a sacrificial bull placed on it. The prophets were then to take turns calling upon their God to bring fire down from heaven to ignite their offering. The God who answered with fire would be declared the true God.

The Baal prophets pleaded from morning till evening. They even lacerated themselves with swords to make blood flow. But Baal did not respond.

Elijah then had four large containers of water poured on his offering. This was repeated twice. After his call to God, fire came down and consumed not only the offering, but also the altar stones and all the water.

Apparently in the Old Testament times, Satanic power was restricted and could not match the power of God to bring fire down from heaven.

Contrast this situation with the prophecies of Revelation concerning the end times and the era of the Antichrist, symbolized by the beast out of the earth.

John describes the beast:

> He performed great and miraculous signs, even causing fire to come down from heaven to earth in full view of men. Because of the signs . . . , he deceived the inhabitants of the earth (Revelation 13:13, 14).

The Bible seems to reveal that in the last days, Satan will be allowed to duplicate powers that were once the special prerogative of the Holy Spirit.

Chapter 13

Secret Infiltration

Jesus had a new mission project for me: I was to secretly infiltrate a local Christian church.

Several months had passed since the start of my mall witnessing and beach ministry. At first, I was not even aware I had started a new mission. Initially, all I was instructed to do was to join the church congregation and take part in as many church activities as possible. After a few weeks, I was given additional instruction. My task was to search for suitable contacts and make friends with them. Then I was to subtly introduce them to the concept of Christian meditation as a means of communion with God. The ultimate goal was to start a meditation group within the congregation.

The new venture began during my mall witnessing activities when I met a dedicated Christian named Wayne. He asked me which church I attended.

"Oh, I am not a member of any one church," I replied. "I regard myself as a member of the body of Christ, and all denominations are part of the body."

"Do you attend a local church?" Wayne asked politely.

"Yes, I have been to several churches in the area. I attend whichever church the spirit leads me to at the time."

Wayne invited me to his own church, Hope Chapel, in Hermosa Beach. I had heard of it, but had never attended there. During my meditation that evening, the inner voice told me to visit this church.

I first visited Hope Chapel for a Sunday evening service attended by about 2,000 people. A band, along with several singers, began the service with contemporary Christian music. The preaching that followed seemed to be based on conservative biblical theology. Although the speaker was gifted, I decided that he obviously needed educating in the more advanced ideas that *Jesus* was bringing to the planet.

A few days later, the inner voice of meditation encouraged me to attend Hope Chapel regularly. I subsequently attended a series of lectures for newcomers to the church, and, after completing it, took a more advanced course required for church membership. The advanced course was taught by a likable member of the pastoral staff named Ken. Being British countrymen, Ken and I became friends.

Up to this time, I had regarded my church attendance as a form of education intended to expand my knowledge of the Christian church. This background enhanced my skill in witnessing to people of various religious persuasions whom I met on the boardwalk at Venice. But now the inner voice of meditation informed me I had a special mission to perform in this particular congregation.

Ginger was my first contact at Hope Chapel. An attractive woman in her early thirties, she played an electric violin in the church band. Having at one time been enthusiastic about the use of electric violins in rock and roll bands, I was most interested in her playing techniques. After the closing song one Sunday evening, I walked up to the stage and congratulated her on her skill. We talked a little about her violin.

A couple of weeks later, I bumped into Ginger in one of the hallways after an evening service. After talking about our mutual appreciation of rock music from the sixties and seventies, our conversation moved to a discussion of our current spiritual lives.

Suddenly the inner voice interjected, "Tell her about your meditation practice."

"Ginger, actually, the main spiritual discipline I practice is meditation," I said with a bit of hesitation.

"Oh, so do I," Ginger replied enthusiastically. "I would go crazy without it."

I felt overjoyed on hearing her statement and didn't even feel the need to elaborate on what I had meant by "meditation." I just sensed that she was obviously talking about the practice of Eastern-type, silent contemplation upon the cosmic. As we talked a little more about our interest in meditation, I suggested that we should start a Christian meditation group at the church. Ginger thought it was a great idea.

At this point, Ken, the British staff pastor, approached and joined us. Even though we were well acquainted, I was hesitant to continue the conversation about meditation. For an instant, I consciously focused inward to listen for any possible warning spoken by my higher self. When there was only silence, I assumed that it must be OK to continue the conversation.

"Ken, we were just discussing the idea of starting a Christian meditation group," I said.

"Hmmm, well, err, err," Ken muttered as a response to my statement.

I interjected, "You know, meditation is spoken of a lot in the Old Testament. David, according to the Psalms, often practiced it as a form of communion with God, a process of listening to the voice of the Holy Spirit. It was also commonly practiced in the monasteries during the Middle Ages, but it has since become a lost art, a victim of the frantic hustle and bustle of modern living."

Ken seemed only mildly interested in what I was saying. He commented casually, "Well, you will have to try to start a group here. I am sure some people will be interested."

Ginger spoke right up, "Yes, I do it myself. It is a

wonderful experience to sit still and relax and give yourself time to be with God."

The prospect of starting a Christian meditation group at Hope Chapel excited me. My desire was to make friends among the church members and to help bring them into a closer relationship with *Jesus*. I regarded myself as part of an effort planned by *Christ* to bring his children into direct communion with himself. Believing that I was a born-again Christian who had a special, direct relationship with *Jesus*, I wanted my Christian "family" to come into that same relationship. I believed that if all Christians would listen to the voice of *Jesus* as I did, then the gospel would be spread quickly, and *the Lord* would soon return permanently as ruler over his kingdom on the planet.

As part of my effort to learn all about Christian doctrines, I frequently visited the local Christian bookstore in my town. Often I amused myself by browsing through the books that attempted to discredit the New Age. Digesting them with interest, I even found them quite entertaining. Even though I considered myself a born-again Christian, I still identified myself as part of the New Age. I believed I possessed the "full gospel," a fusion between Christianity and New Age ideas.

As I read the anti–New Age books written by my Christian "brothers," I wished I could persuade the authors that no real conflict existed. I wanted them to understand that the New Age and Christianity were just separate arms of *God's* great plan to reconcile himself with mankind.

Even though I regarded myself as a New Ager, the inner voice prohibited me from confiding this to anyone. During my ministry activities at Venice Beach, I often passed peddlers selling New Age jewelry and music. I wanted to stop and share with them the fact that I was New Ager. However, each time I tried to approach them, my higher self immediately interjected, "No. Don't do it."

It was as if I were allowed to present only a *Christian* image to all the people I met.

Jeff was another friend I met at Hope Chapel. A bright young man in his late teens, he loved to tell people he met about the Lord. My accounts of mystical experiences resulting from practicing *Christian* meditation fascinated him.

Wayne, the man who first told me about Hope Chapel, was another totally devoted Christian whom I tried to influence. He constantly carried his Bible and loved to share the Word of God with people he met. We, too, became good friends.

I told Wayne that his studying of the Word was an excellent activity, but I stressed that something far greater than the Scriptures was available.

He became excited when I told him that he could actually practice the presence of *God* and listen to the voice of the *Holy Spirit*. I backed my claim by reminding him that Jesus told his disciples that the kingdom was within them.

Marantz.

The word was on my mind as soon as I woke up in the morning. Marantz? What is Marantz? I had never heard the word before.

During breakfast, the word kept popping into my mind. I thought, Perhaps it is the name of a new car model I heard advertised on the radio.

Racking my brain as to what Marantz was, I finally concluded it must be a new model of Japanese car. I began to wonder if it was an omen from *God* that I would soon need to purchase a new car.

Later that day I went to Hope Chapel for the evening service. As I glanced at the church bulletin's advertisement page, an ominous shiver ran down my spine as I read the first line.

Marantz

Marantz stereo for sale. . . .

"Wow, the *Holy Spirit* has been at work again," I exclaimed, knowing that the name Marantz had been planted in my mind the previous night. I regarded the occurrence as an indication from the *Holy Spirit* that I needed to contact the person advertising the stereo.

I called up the guy and asked him about the stereo. Telling me his name was Greg, he asked me to come over to his place to inspect the Marantz system.

As I entered his apartment, I scanned the room for any clues as to why I had been sent there, clues such as New Age books. I focused on a large book on the table—a book about India. Hmmm, I thought, interesting.

The inner voice told me not to purchase the stereo, but rather to just become acquainted with Greg. During our long and friendly conversation, I began to speculate whether he was destined to be part of the meditation group I aspired to start in the church.

Shortly after the visit with Greg, my clandestine mission to infiltrate Hope Chapel with New Age teachings came to a sudden and abrupt halt. My parents—long suspecting that I was involved in a questionable religion—had been praying for me for a long time. A stranger in a gospel meeting also prayed for me at a very critical time. These prayers promoted a strange move of the Holy Spirit, which resulted in my experiencing a dramatic and unexpected "illumination." The result was incredible: My twelve-year relationship with the New Age fell apart in one gigantic crash as the Mastermind's ugly web of deception was torn asunder.

Chapter 14

Unmasking the Mastermind

"Do not go," the voice of conscience exhorted.

After work, I was planning to attend a special evangelistic rally.

"Tonight you have to witness for me in the mall," the voice commanded.

Strongly wanting to go to the rally, I decided to ignore the inner voice.

A tension had been building inside of me for a couple of weeks. I could sense that *Jesus Christ* wanted me to devote even more time and effort to his ministry work. And yet a rebelliousness started to grow inside me, as if another force countering the instructions from *Jesus* were coming into play.

Rebelling against my voice of conscience, I attended the evangelist's meeting. It was held in the large auditorium of a local college.

During the meeting I was seated next to a woman who looked to be in her thirties. At the end of the event she asked me in a soft voice, "Have you enjoyed the evangelist's talk?"

"Yes, he's pretty good," I replied, "but I find his view to be very narrow-minded."

The truth was that I had felt very uncomfortable during the preacher's talk. By the time it was over, I was boiling with agitation against his fundamentalist stance and was determined to start being bold and open about my New Age–oriented beliefs. I decided that I had to counteract these heresies preached by the fundamentalists in the name of my master.

The woman asked calmly, "What kind of religious views do you have?"

"I am a New Age Christian," I blurted out.

This was the first time I had made such a statement to a Christian believer. The inner voice of conscience had always cautioned me not be open about my New Age beliefs. But after hearing the evangelist, I was angry and unwilling to be silent any longer. Unwittingly the preacher had fanned the flames of my passion and courage.

To my surprise, the woman did not express any disgust at my answer. "Oh," she commented humbly, "I used to be involved with the New Age myself, until I came to the Lord."

From the way she expressed herself, I sensed that she no longer approved of the New Age.

"Well, you shouldn't feel bad about it," I said frankly. "The New Age has some excellent ideas and truths. Most of the New Agers just lack the direct power of *Jesus Christ* in their lives."

When she didn't answer, I asked politely, "Which church do you attend?"

"The Church on the Way."

"Oh yes," I interrupted, "Jack Hayford's place. I know about it. I have never been there, but I sometimes listen to Jack on the radio."

"Concerning this New Age Christianity you are involved in," said the woman, "do you mind if I pray for you right now? I do not know what you believe, but I would like to pray for you."

"Yeah, sure, we can pray," I replied, thinking that I could always use extra prayers to help me in my ministry work.

The woman took hold of my hand as we prayed. "Dear Heavenly Father," she began. "I ask that you will give this brother wisdom to perceive that which is true. Let him fully understand your Word. I ask that the mighty power of the Holy Spirit will be at work in his life, leading him to a true knowledge of Jesus. I ask this in Jesus' name. Amen."

How nice to be prayed for, I thought to myself as I left the auditorium. Even though I have a close relationship with *Jesus*, I would like to be filled with more of his power and truth.

About a week after the gospel rally, I was preparing to quit work at the end of the day. "Do not go to the library," the inner voice instructed. "You must witness in the mall this evening."

I remained aloof to the unwelcome voice of conscience.

"You have to do my work," it commanded sternly, as if expressing the words of *Jesus*. "Time is running out. You have to get your ministry established."

The spirit of rebelliousness against the inner voice rose again. On this particular evening, I stubbornly continued to ignore the prompting. An alternative project loomed in the forefront of my mind: I wanted to read a particular book. Even though the inner voice kept exhorting me to do mall witnessing, I determined to obtain a copy of this book.

In my earlier study of Gordon Melton's *Encyclopedia of American Religions*, I had read an interesting section describing a woman who claimed to have had visions from God during the middle of the nineteenth century. The idea that a Christian mystic lived before the time of Madam Blavatski and Alice Bailey stimulated my deep interest. It sounded as if she may well have been a New Age Christian living decades before the start of the contemporary New Age movement.

From a library I borrowed *Ellen G. White, Prophet of Destiny* by Rene Noorbergen.[1]

---

1. Keats Publishing, 1972.

It began by describing a vision in which Ellen White saw the 1906 San Francisco earthquake several days before its actual occurrence.[2] The apparent psychic ability was impressive and encouraged me to read on.

A general discussion followed concerning the difference between psychic ability and prophecy. The author analyzed psychic mediums such as Edgar Case, Jeane Dixon, and Peter Hurkos from the standpoint of comparing their teachings with biblical Scripture. Then followed a short biography of Ellen White's early life.

My attention was then drawn to the chapter "Unmasking the Mastermind" containing Ellen White's narrative of a vision she had in 1858.[3]

She wrote:

> The Lord has shown me that Satan was once an honored angel in heaven, . . . next to Christ. His countenance, like those of the other angels, was mild and expressive of happiness. His forehead was high and broad, showing great intelligence. His form was perfect; his bearing noble and majestic. But when God said to his Son, "Let us make man in our image," Satan was jealous of Jesus. He wished to be consulted concerning the formation of man, and because he was not, he was filled with envy, jealousy and hatred. He desired to receive the highest honors in heaven next to God.

I wondered whether there really was a Satan who rebelled in heaven with a bunch of evil angels. I remem-

---

2. Ellen White was the daughter of a lay preacher and was brought up as a strict Methodist. She claimed to have had her first vision in 1844. In 1863, she co-founded the Seventh-day Adventist Church as a formal denomination.

3. The vision is known as the Great Controversy Vision.

bered that Muriel sometimes talked about Satan and negative forces; she seemed to think he was a real being. Djwhal Khul, on the other hand, denounced the idea that a great enemy of God existed; he considered the devil to be a fictitious myth.

Ellen White's narrative drew my attention again.

> Until this time, . . . all heaven had been in order, harmony and perfect subjection to the government of God. It was the highest sin to rebel against His order and will. All heaven seemed in commotion. . . . There was contention among the angels. Satan and his sympathizers were striving to reform the government of God. They wished to look into His unsearchable wisdom and ascertain His purpose in exalting Jesus and endowing Him with such unlimited power and command. They rebelled against the authority of the Son. All the heavenly host were summoned to appear before the Father to have each case decided. It was there determined that Satan should be expelled from heaven, with all the angels who had joined him in the rebellion.

I began to consider that maybe there really was an archangel in heaven called Satan who became jealous and rebelled against God. Perhaps Satan existed somewhere upon our planet in the realm of the spirit planes.

I read on.

> Satan stood in amazement at his new condition. His happiness was gone. He looked upon the angels who, with him, were once so happy, but who had been expelled from heaven with him. Before their fall not a shade of discontent had marred their perfect bliss. Now all seemed changed. Countenances which had reflected the image of their Maker were gloomy and despair-

ing. Strife, discord, and bitter recrimination were among them. . . .

When Satan became fully conscious that there was no possibility of his being brought again into favor with God, his malice and hatred began to manifest. He consulted with his angels, and a plan was laid to still work against God's government. When Adam and Eve were placed in the beautiful garden, Satan was laying plans to destroy them. It was decided that Satan should assume another form and manifest an interest for man. He must insinuate against God's truthfulness and create doubt whether God did mean just what He said.

Putting the book down, I contemplated on this fascinating account of the rebellion. Did Satan really rebel and then feel gloom and despair in his separation from God?

I picked up the book again and continued to read.

Satan commenced his work with Eve, to cause her to disobey. . . . As soon as Eve had disobeyed she became a powerful medium through which to occasion the fall of her husband. . . .

. . . Then Satan exulted. . . .

The news of man's fall spread through heaven. Every harp was hushed. The angels cast their crowns from their heads in sorrow. All heaven was in agitation. . . .

. . . Satan triumphed. He had made others suffer by his fall. He had been shut out of heaven . . . they out of paradise.

Wondering whether there had been an Adam and Eve who were tempted by the devil in Paradise, I recalled that, as a Christian teenager, I had accepted the teaching that life started with God's creation as recorded in Genesis. But for some reason, I had discounted the idea that Adam and Eve were tempted and fell. It was as if I didn't want to believe in a Satan who could tempt people. I felt more at ease with the idea that temptation was an internal process occurring within a person's psyche caused by foolishness and ignorance.

I recalled that Muriel believed in the Genesis account of the fall. Based upon revelations from *Jesus*, she told us that Eve's sin was a terrible catastrophe and subsequently caused all the suffering we now find on the planet.

I returned to Ellen White's narrative.

> He [Jesus] then made known to the angelic host that a way of escape had been made for lost man. He told them that He had been pleading with His Father, and had offered to give His life as a ransom, to take the sentence of death upon Himself, that through Him man might find pardon; that through the merits of His blood, and obedience to the law of God, they could have the favor of God, and be brought into the beautiful garden, and eat of the fruit of the tree of life.
>
> At first the angels could not rejoice; for their Commander concealed nothing from them, but opened before them the plan of salvation. Jesus told them that He would stand between the wrath of His Father and guilty man, that He would bear iniquity and scorn, and but few would receive Him as the Son of God. Nearly all would hate and reject Him.

Resting my eyes for a moment, I thought, So this was how the beloved Jesus planned to redeem mankind: He offered to take on the karma of the world and pay the price by his own death. Amazing.

I was anxious to read on.

> He would leave all glory in heaven, appear

upon earth as a man, humble Himself as a man, become acquainted by His own experience with the various temptations with which man would be beset, that He might know how to succor those who should be tempted; and that finally, after His mission as a teacher would be accomplished, He would be delivered into the hands of men, and endure almost every cruelty and suffering that Satan and his angels could inspire wicked men to inflict; that He would die the cruelest of deaths, hung between the heavens and the earth, as a guilty sinner; that He would suffer dreadful hours of agony, which even angels could not look upon, but would veil their faces from the sight. Not merely agony of body would He suffer, but mental agony, that with which bodily suffering could in no wise be compared. The weight of the sins of the whole world would be upon Him. He told them He would die and rise again the third day, and would ascend to His Father to intercede for wayward, guilty man. . . .

With a holy sadness Jesus comforted and cheered the angels and informed them that hereafter those whom He should redeem would be with Him, and that by His death He should ransom many and destroy him who had the power of death. And His Father would give Him the kingdom . . . under the whole heaven, and He would possess it forever and ever. Satan and sinners would be destroyed, nevermore to disturb heaven or the purified new earth.

I felt a sense of admiration and awe as I appreciated the task that Jesus had accomplished. Turning back to the book, I read further:

I was shown Satan as he once was, a happy,

exalted angel. Then I was shown him as he now is. He still bears a kingly form. His features are still noble, for he is an angel fallen. But the expression of his countenance is full of anxiety, care, unhappiness, malice, hate, mischief, deceit, and every evil. That brow which was once so noble, I particularly noticed. His forehead commenced from his eyes to recede. I saw that he had so long bent himself to evil that every good quality was debased, and every evil trait was developed. His eyes were cunning, sly, and showed great penetration. His frame was large, but the flesh hung loosely about his hands and face. As I beheld him, his chin was resting upon his left hand. He appeared to be in deep thought. A smile was upon his countenance, which made me tremble, it was so full of evil and satanic slyness.

In my imagination I pictured the image of Satan as described by Ellen White. Suddenly I felt devastated and weak with a monumental realization.

"It is him," I gasped aloud. "It is my master."

"I have been a follower of Satan all these years."

Feeling as if I had been thrown out of an airplane without a parachute, I shuddered in anguish as my whole world collapsed before me.

As I again imaged the evil, sly smile upon Satan's countenance, a horrifying thought pierced my mind: I had been watching him set up his New Age, counterfeit Christianity; his final trump card would be for him to appear on our planet in a physical body and claim to be Jesus Christ—the New Age "reappearance of the Christ."

"Oh, God!" I exclaimed in shock and agony. "Djwhal Khul and *Jesus Christ* are Satan's evil angels. They have been deceiving me all these years." There was no doubt about it in my mind: I had been a disciple of Satan; the whole New Age movement and its counterfeit Christianity is a clever plan by Satan to thwart the mission of true Christianity. I suddenly understood that Satan is ultimately preparing the world for his spectacular appearance in which millions and millions of people will proclaim him to be Christ, the returned Messiah. In reality it will be the appearing of the Antichrist.

A biblical text flashed into my mind: "False Christs and false prophets will appear . . . to deceive even the elect—if that were possible."

Devastated with anguish, I was inundated with one horrifying insight after another: Satan and his angels had been training me to be a false prophet. I had become their slave. All those so-called masters of the Hierarchy have never lived as evolved humans in the Himalayas or anywhere else. The masters and the other New Age spirit guides are nothing more than Satan's angels masquerading as agents of God; they are the very angels who were thrown out of heaven at the time of Satan's great rebellion.

Thinking back to the incredible visitation of Djwhal Kuhl some six years before, I realized that I had been completely fooled by the brilliance of his appearance and the claim that he was a 350-year-old Tibetan guru who had finally reached immortality after several incarnations upon this planet. I was shattered to know that Djwhal Kuhl had never ever lived as a human being, but was, in fact, a satanic angel.

I realized that, as an angel, Djwhal Khul had the power to take on a human form and appear as a man, even looking like Jesus Christ. He could appear in his etheric "light body" as he had appeared to me; or he could appear in a physical, flesh-and-blood body, as he had first appeared to Muriel in 1963.

Feeling like a person who has just received news of the death of a spouse, I was stunned into motionless silence.

Thoughts began welling up in my mind concerning all the money and time I had devoted to the New Age movement, all the hours spent in meditation and study. It was all for nothing. All that had been achieved was to ensure my eternal destruction by the fires of hell. All my endeavors to lead people to *Jesus Christ* and New Age *Christianity* were simply maneuvers to bring them on the road leading to everlasting death.

I now accepted the real biblical Jesus. The rapidity of my conviction paralleled several convictions recorded in the book of Acts—the conversion of 3,000 in one day after Pentecost, Saul's encounter on the road to Damascus, and the conversion of the Philippian jailer.

Sitting in motionless introspection for hours, I found the memory banks of my mind flooding open like a bursting dam. I began to review my youth and remembered the long-forgotten steps I had taken that slowly led away from Christian teachings and brought me into the world of mysticism and the occult.

Suddenly, a profound memory surfaced that made me aghast at its implications. The memory concerned a visit I had made as a youth to a movie theater showing a certain film about devil worship. I had completely forgotten this event in my life, as if the memory had been buried deep in my subconscious. In the trauma of my dramatic exit from the New Age, the memory surfaced with vivid clarity and detail.

I was fifteen years old at the time, and life seemed some-what boring. Everyone portrayed on TV seemed to live a dynamic and interesting existence. This created a desire for excitement to counteract the mundane rut I perceived myself to be in.

Across from my high school was a theater specializing in horror movies, generally of the Frankenstein type. Looking at the posters, I used to think how exciting it would be to see some of these films that were too grisly to be shown on television. Disobeying the counsel of my parents, I visited the theater on several occasions.

Remembering clearly the scenes from this specific devil-worship movie, I was shocked to realize that this film was directly responsible for starting me on the road to the real world of the occult.

The movie *The Devil Rides Out* had two main characters. The leading character was a young man who was being lured into a group of devil worshipers. His antagonist was a modern-day Magus, or occult magician. The Magus—the "good" man in the plot—was attempting to rescue the young man from his involvement with influential satanists.

The devil worshipers were a group of rich aristocrats and powerful businessmen. At prearranged times, they met at a remote, country estate to participate in various satanic rites and rituals designed to enhance their wealth, power, and social standing.

The crisis in the film centered on a major festival planned by the Satan worshipers, during which they planned to invoke the personal presence of the devil himself, so that he would bless them with even greater power and wealth. As part of the festival, the young man was scheduled to be ceremonially initiated into full membership of the satanic lodge.

The film showed the members of this satanic cult arriving at the worship scene in beautiful antique Rolls Royces, with paint and chrome glistening like diamonds. A large bonfire was burning in a forest clearing. Near the fire, they erected an altar dedicated to Satan.

The movie depicted the Magus—planning to orchestrate a dramatic rescue of the young man—performing ritual magic to protect himself from the power of Satan. He centered himself inside a large astrological horoscope drawn on the floor of a room in his mansion. He performed various prayers and incantations, using a crucifix and other mystic paraphernalia in the process. He lighted large candles and recited various occult mantras, even quoting some biblical-sounding texts.

I can remember being deeply fascinated by the film. As a bored teenager, the exciting lifestyle and drama depicted in the film scenes especially intrigued me. It was easy to be drawn by the lavish wealth and the beautiful women possessed by the lodge members. The exciting activities of the Magus, with all his mystical paraphernalia, were equally stimulating and intriguing.

Sitting in deep introspection as I vividly remembered the scenes from the movie, I realized in horror that something subtle and sinister had happened to me as I watched that film. A powerful seed of fascination with the occult and the mystical had been sown in my own psyche. The seed did not germinate for several years. But it was deeply rooted and gradually drew me into the enchanting world of mysticism and the occult.

As I focused on the memory of the movie, I had the powerful insight that, as a teenager, my absorption with the film started a definite relationship with Satan. I had subtly crossed over a subconscious threshold in which my inner nature accepted the idea of mysticism as a means of gaining personal power. I was primed and ready to later enthusiastically swallow Satan's lure of New Age metaphysics.

I shudder when I think about what is happening in the movie theaters of today. Films about the occult and the mystical are commonplace. Even such apparently innocuous episodes as *E.T.* and *Star Wars* are seeped in occult and mystical concepts. For example, it is known that George Lucas, the creator of the *Star Wars* trilogy of films, was heavily influenced by Carlos Castaneda's book *Tales of Power.*[4] Castaneda's account of the Mexican Indian sorcerer, Don Juan, was a book that strongly motivated me to search for New Age shamans in Los Angeles.

How ironic that the "good" character in the film *The Devil Rides Out* was actually every bit as satanic as the devil worshipers themselves, the supposedly "evil" people

---

4. *The Reincarnation Sensation*, p. 16, by N. L. Geisler and J. Y. Amano, Tyndale House, 1986.

in the plot. Today I can see how Satan uses his brilliant intellect to deceive New Agers into believing that they are "good" guys trying to spread light and wisdom in an evil world of ignorance.

The devil has scored a major publicity victory by inspiring the media to represent him as a loathsome, fictitious being having the form of an ugly beast. *The Devil Rides Out* portrayed Satan as a beast with the body of a man and the head of a bull. Other common images picture Satan as a red ghoulish devil with horns, wearing a black cape and holding a pitchfork. This image is so bizarre that most people have totally discounted Satan's real existence and regard him as a purely mythical figure. Even though I was brought up as a Christian, I did not believe that Satan existed. Few people are aware of Satan's true existence and identity: an angel of light looking similar to how one would expect Jesus Christ to look.

If people do not stand firmly behind the truth of the Bible as the inerrant Word of God, they are easily led astray when Satan appears in his shining angelic form. They automatically think that the great being of light in front of them is Jesus Christ—or at least one of God's great angels—no matter what unbiblical ideas the false messenger begins to propound.

When the same manifestation occurs to New Age apostles, they are stimulated to teach philosophies of greater deception. Take, for example, Paramahansa Yogananda, the guru founder of the USA–based Hindu/Christian sect, Self Realization Fellowship. When a satanic angel visited him and masqueraded as Jesus Christ, Yogananda incorporated *Christianity* into his pagan Hindu religion, thereby making it simultaneously more devious and acceptable to Westerners. By this maneuver, even more people could be led astray.

When you consider, for example, 54 percent of the clergy of a major mainline denomination do not believe that the devil is a personal being who directs evil forces, then it is no wonder people will be led astray by signs, wonders, and miracles.[5] For if they reject the idea of Satan's existence, they assume that all miraculous and wondrous religious manifestations must come from God.

Even if a person believes in Satan's existence, the visit from an angelic being tends to so inflate one's ego that he is reluctant to consider the possibility that the mysterious visitor is other than a divine being sent from God.

For a couple of weeks after the realization that I had been a disciple of Satan, I was awash with memories of how as a child and adolescent I had become more and more rebellious against Christian teachings and the good qualities of my character. For instance, I started to curse and use obscene language in order to blend in with the habits of my play friends. Eventually I was so immersed in sin and worldliness that the devil was able to take control of my life and lead me into his domain.

Later I had mistakenly believed that my subsequent entry into "mystical Christianity" was a venture bringing me toward greater godliness and peace. Instead, I was actually being lured deeper and deeper into the Mastermind's evil trap.

I recoil in horror as I think about what would have happened to me at the second coming of Christ if I had not been rescued from my counterfeit beliefs. When the trumpet sounded, the mighty earthquake shook, and the host of heavenly angels appeared, I would have considered myself ready and eager for the rapture. Then would have followed the terrible devastation as I discovered I was not being taken up. I would have claimed in desperation, "Lord, Lord, did I not preach in your name; did not miracles and signs and wonders appear in my life?"

Imagine the excruciating shock to hear the words, "I never knew you. Away from me, you evildoer."

---

5. Gallop survey published in *Christianity Today*, June 6, 1980.

After my rescue from Satan's darkness, I was so glad to have found deliverance and to know the true Jesus Christ, his mission, and his sacrifice on the cross. Instead of being a false apostle, I now joined Christian congregations as a repenting sinner.

I apologized to my Christian contacts for trying to lead them astray. After I told them of my former identity and story, they were amazed to learn I had been a Bible-carrying disciple of Satan. They were not aware that they had been targets of the secret invasion.

I was so shaken at the time of my departure from the occult, I had to seek counseling support from Christian pastors and educators. Several weeks of trauma passed before I started to feel confidence in victory over Satan's counterattacks of intimidation and harassment.

My exit from Satan's web of deception not only involved drastic changes in my religious beliefs; I actually noticed quite marked changes in my physiology.

For example, I had always regarded the stereo in my new car to perform poorly in spite of its being an expensive unit. The system seemed to lack bass tones. I had taken the car in to have the sound system repaired, but without success.

A couple of weeks after ceasing all meditation and metaphysical activity, I noticed I could hear rich, deep bass tones on my car stereo. It seems as if my total bondage of slavery to Satan had actually produced changes in my physiology. These changes seemed to reverse when I became a follower of the real, biblical Jesus and stopped my meditation activities.

I now regard deep involvement in New Age consciousness-raising techniques to act somewhat as a cocaine of the mind. For example, after my exit from the New Age, I noticed that for about a month I felt oversensitive to stimulus. For instance, the noise of a crowded restaurant bothered me a great deal. It was as if I were suffering from "cold turkey" withdrawal symptoms. I concluded that the prolonged use of meditation techniques actually produced subtle changes within my brain, as if I had been absorbing a type of psychic cocaine during meditation. It took a couple of months before I felt normal.

Upon my return to the body of Christ, a lot of my thinking had to be reprogrammed. I had been so deeply indoctrinated into the ideas of metaphysics that I was sometimes unsure if an idea was biblical, or if it was something that I had absorbed during New Age training and study.

I was relieved to be rescued. Satan's angels had made my life a nightmare of oppression. Having taken over my voice of conscience, they could interject into my mind and influence my emotions at any time, thereby making me a slave to their demands. When the slavery was broken, I rejoiced in the release of freedom of choice.

I am so thankful to God for sending the Holy Spirit to inspire me to read something that broke the Mastermind's power. I attribute the action of the Holy Spirit to be in response to the earnest prayers of devoted Christians, particularly my parents, who had suspected I was being deceived and who had diligently spent years praying for my deliverance. For their prayers, I am humbly thankful. For the special prayer by the woman from Jack Hayford's church, I am grateful.

I thank God I am saved through the love and grace of Jesus Christ. I am thankful for his word, the Bible, and for the power of prayer that reveals truth and protects us from deception and evil. I am thankful for the assurance of one day being with God in his glorious heaven and reigning with him on the new earth.

I say with Paul, "The Lord will rescue me . . . and will bring me safely to his heavenly kingdom. To him be glory for ever and ever" (2 Timothy 4:18).

I rejoice that I have personally experienced the fulfillment of Jesus' promise that "the truth will set you free" (John 8:32).

Appendix 1

Perspectives on the New Age Movement

As a former New Ager who is now a Christian, how do I view the New Age?

In essence, I regard the New Age as a counterfeit system of religion devised by Satan to be an attractive alternative to Bible-based Christianity. Its ultimate goal is to lead the churches into a great apostasy in preparation for the appearance of the Antichrist, so that he will be accepted as the Messiah by both *Christians* and New Agers alike.

At its core, New Age is primarily based on Hindu philosophy suitably adapted for the Western culture. Satan has cleverly repackaged Hinduism into a form devoid of the fearful, repulsive deities who are endlessly placated in the traditional Hindu rituals. Instead of advocating a plethora of grotesque gods, the New Age focuses on a single, pantheistic god, who is presented as being the same god as the Father Most High of the Judeo-Christian tradition.

In the New Age religion, the Hindu teachings are combined with ancient paganism, contemporary occultism, spiritualism, and Christianity to produce a multifaceted hodgepodge of deceit.

The pagan elements include astrology, numerology, tarot, kabala, and various other divination methods. These practices generally originated in Babylon and

Egypt during the Old Testament era and were expressly forbidden by the Bible.

The contemporary Western occult element derives from such sources as Theosophy and Rosicrucianism, both much colored by ancient paganism. New Age occultism now incorporates more modern pseudoscientific activity into its repertoire, such as found in the current New Age fascination with crystals, auras, UFOs, and parapsychology (ESP).

The spiritualism element, especially New Age channeling, adds a dynamic and sensational aspect to the New Age. The apparent ability of mediums to contact the spirits of deceased relatives and great spirit guides convinces the New Age followers that the spirit world is a realm of reality. And of course it is, except that the spirits the medium contacts are not the benevolent entities the followers think they are.

Many New Age organizations emphasize only one, or possibly just a select few, of the various branches of New Age knowledge and activity. Frequently New Age groups even advocate competing philosophies, but this conflict does not really create a problem for Satan. Because the philosophies are all deception, it doesn't matter if the various groups have conflicting ideas, as long as potential victims will find one of them attractive.

The New Age movement is not a clearly defined organization. It is a blanket term used to denote the collective existence of all the organizations and individuals promoting the New Age philosophies. It has no single human leader or umbrella administration.

Satan is well aware that a clearly defined, single organization with homogeneous philosophies would have a serious drawback. Its critics could easily confront and expose it as a fraudulent system masquerading under the auspices of divinity. To avoid this disclosure, Satan appears to have deliberately organized his counterfeit religion by the network concept. Under this model, thousands of organizations exist independently under the New Age identity, each organization being responsible for its own particular blend of teachings.

Many allied organizations also share similar ideas to mainstream New Age, but do not even call themselves New Age or use that term in their general vocabulary. Examples are the Unity School of Christianity, Christian Science (Church of Christ, Scientist), and Scientology (L. Ron Hubbard's Dianetics).

Satan has set up his New Age movement with such a multitude of teachings and practices available that at least one of them is bound to appeal to almost anyone. Thus, if financial success attracts a person, the variety of human potential seminars could start him on the process of being led into Satan's domain. Perhaps a certain person would not be drawn by channeling, but hatha yoga exercises may sound interesting and useful. The hatha yoga could then lead to meditation, which could eventually lead to channeling, the activity of which the person was originally wary. Some people start by reading simple astrology predictions in their daily newspaper.

You may ask what Satan's motive is for setting up counterfeit religions such as Hinduism and the New Age. It would seem that Satan wants everyone to be an atheist.

Satan probably has several motives. One of them, I am sure, is survival. The counterfeit religions provide severe competition against the spread of the Christian gospel message, thus extending Satan's time. However, I think the most fundamental motive for Satan's promotion of counterfeit religions is aptly described by the prophet Isaiah:

> You said in your heart,
> "I will ascend to heaven;
> I will raise my throne above the stars of God;
> I will sit enthroned on the mount of assembly,
>   on the utmost heights of the sacred mountain.

I will ascend above the tops of the clouds;
I will make myself like the Most High" (Isaiah 14:13,
  14).

Satan desired and coveted God's position in heaven.
On the human level, this sin of covetousness, which
caused Lucifer's fall, is denounced by the tenth commandment. Counterfeit religions are an avenue whereby
Satan now receives worship, just as if he were a god.

It seems more than chance that one of the main
tenets of Hinduism and the New Age is the concept that
humans are gods in the making. By emphasizing this
philosophy, Satan appears to be projecting his own
desires onto the motives of human beings. At the beginning of human history in the Garden of Eden, Satan
was busy pushing the same temptation. During the
world's first channeling session, Satan, the master spirit
guide, used a serpent as his first medium and communicated to Eve, "Your eyes will be opened [you will
have enlightenment], and you will be like God [have cosmic consciousness]" (Genesis 3:4).

Not only does Satan's Hinduism ascribe to the idea
that the goal of man is to become a god, it also claims
that the great gurus of India were literally god incarnated in human flesh. Thus it seeks to confer the status
of Christ upon its prime leaders, those supergurus
known as avatars. Even some New Agers believe that
they themselves are gods and are thus free to create
their own code of moral conduct and belief system,
rather than abide by the code and faith given to
mankind in the Bible.

New Age "Christianity"

One way for Satan to make his New Age more acceptable to Christians is to "Christianize" it. The "conversion" of the Lighted Way is an example of an attempt to
cloak the New Age in a Christian disguise, thus making
it more effective in influencing Christians.

However, I do not think Satan will "convert" all New Age centers into counterfeit Christian churches. Probably most New Age centers will retain the emphasis on traditional metaphysical teachings. Only time will reveal whether Satan has a general plan to give other New Age centers a Christian flavor.

Regarding what happened at the Lighted Way, it appears that Satan's angels deliberately put it through a bogus conversion because they decided its best mission was to act as a counterfeit Christian church, engaged in the task of leading Christians and potential Christians into false doctrines and dangerous meditation practices. The fact that we really believed we were Christians made us potentially more effective for that task.

To a counterfeit Christian, the idea of Satan's existence can itself be quite acceptable. Satan's work is conveniently pointed out as evident elsewhere—in atheism, secret occult groups, drugs, crime, or the actual Church of Satan. It is less easy to believe that Satan expresses himself through organizations and people calling themselves "Christian."

As a New Age "Christian," I had read those biblical passages that warned against false prophets and teachings. But I never seriously considered that I was involved with them. The deception was possible because I did not believe that the *whole* Bible should be understood just exactly as it is written. Because of this, I was able to compromise and embrace false teachings while knowing that they contradicted plain Scripture.

We need to pray in earnest for ourselves, for our Christian family, and for our church leaders, that we will not be led into false doctrines by deceiving spirits and their followers. Paul warned us about this trend in his letter to Timothy:

> The time will come when men will not put up with sound doctrine. Instead, to suit their own desires, they will gather around them a great

number of teachers to say what their itching ears want to hear. They will turn their ears away from the truth and turn aside to myths (2 Timothy 4:3, 4).

Appendix 2

The Psychic Power of Satan

Can Meditation Be Christian?

Several months ago I gave a talk to the staff of a Christian media center that produced television and radio programs. After my presentation, I was shocked to hear a staff member inform me that not too long before, a visiting executive from a seminary had given them a lecture on the virtues of meditation. He then coerced his audience into sitting in silence with their eyes closed so they could listen to the "voice of the Holy Spirit."

Another seminary teacher promotes meditation with the motto: "If you spend an hour praying to God, doesn't it make sense to spend another hour in meditation listening for his reply?" A well-known miracle healer also enthusiastically promotes meditation. He describes meditation as an act of listening to the inner voice of *God.*

These theologians and preachers advocate a type of meditation in which one deliberately sits in introspective silence, attempting to listen to the voice of the Holy Spirit. Before I explain why I consider this so-called Christian meditation to be dangerous, let's take a look at the nature of introspective meditation.

At a New Age seminar given by a Christian lecturer, I heard the statement that New Agers enter into an "altered state" of consciousness when they meditate. The idea that meditation is an "altered state" has been expressed by others involved in ministering to Eastern cults. I believe this view is accurate, but must clarify the point that "altered state" does not necessarily mean "mystical state."

Sometimes people can indeed have mystical experiences during meditation, and they will have been in a tangible, altered state of consciousness. However, from my own experiences and from a knowledge of the experiences of other New Agers, these mystical experiences are not the norm. In fact, I know of New Agers who have meditated for years and have never had a "mystical" experience. It is my assessment that meditation is typically a state of special relaxation and not a radically altered state of consciousness.

I make these points because Christians often believe that meditation is fine as long as it is not done in a mystical state. As most New Age meditation is nonmystical, this argument has no validity.

If meditation is not a mystical state, why is it inappropriate for Christians?

The danger of introspective meditation lies in the fact that the meditator is ready and receptive for an angelic entity to implant thoughts, ideas, and impressions into his mind. From my personal experience, I believe that Satanic angels are able to telepathically implant thoughts into a meditator's mind without the necessity of any mystical state. The meditator simply experiences inspirational thoughts or images materializing in his conscience, which he regards as originating from his "higher self," supposedly a part of his mind that holds communion with God.

I believe it is impossible for anyone to know for sure that a certain impression received during meditation comes from God and not from some other source. Meditation provides an excellent opportunity for Satan to exercise his manipulating deception. Why else would New Agers be promoting it so heavily?

My mall and beach ministry focused on encouraging

individuals to begin the practice of *Christian* meditation. My goal when infiltrating Hope Chapel was to start a *Christian* meditation group in that church. I took comfort in the knowledge that once people started to meditate, they would hear the inner voice of *God* inside of their own minds, and this would lead them into the arena of other New Age ideas.

What Does the Bible Say About Meditation?

In order to help convince people of the benefits of meditation, I decided to write a small booklet on *Christian* meditation and the Bible. I was sure that I could use several texts as a support for my thesis. Researching my Bible thoroughly, I was surprised that I could not find a single instance in the Bible in which someone sat down in silent meditation, waiting for the voice of God to give him instructions.

Instead, taken in its context, every use of the term *meditation* in the Bible evoked a meaning of thought and contemplation on the scriptural Word of God or on God's divine qualities. Most references are found in the Psalms.

In each instance that the psalmist used the term *meditation*, it referred to his intellectual contemplation on Scripture and the way it revealed the character of God. One example: "I will meditate on your precepts" (Psalm 119:78). Never did the context hint that David was directly listening to the voice of God in the silence of self-hypnosis.

Not one single Old Testament prophet commented that he sat down in silence and had to strain himself to quiet his mind in order to hear the voice of God "within" give him a message. In each case of prophetic communication, God took the initiative and directly approached the prophet.

Using contextual Scripture as a reference, I was unable to write the booklet. I then decided to use scriptural verses out of context to bolster my argument advocating meditation for the Christian.

Had I checked my local Christian bookstore, I could have saved myself the trouble of planning my publication. A book already in wide circulation—*The Other Side of Silence: A Guide to Christian Meditation*, by Morton T. Kelsey—promoted *Christian* meditation. Commonly used as a textbook in theology classes, the book has sold over 100,000 copies. Ironically, the book contains numerous references to New Age writers. For example, the first author on Kelsey's acknowledgments list is Roberto Assagioli, M.D. He is the founder of psychosynthesis, a popular New Age workshop topic. A pioneer within the New Age movement, Assagioli often quotes from Alice Bailey's Djwhal Kuhl occult teachings.

Honest research will reveal that meditation of the Eastern type has no biblical or historical basis in the Christian church. To my knowledge, no record exists of the apostles, the postapostolic fathers, or the great reformers, such as Luther, Calvin, Tyndale, or Wesley, having practiced it.

Introspective meditation can be viewed as a potential hot line leading directly to the mind of Satan. No doubt most preachers who promote it are sincere but are nevertheless misguided and in danger of becoming agents of Satan, if they are not so already.

For me, the appropriate Christian devotional practice, the one the Bible encourages, is to contemplate upon the Scriptures and pray earnestly.

Mystical Experiences

When New Agers have mystical experiences during their meditation, I don't believe that the meditator has the power in himself to produce that experience, such as willing himself into a deeper, altered state of consciousness. It is my opinion that a satanic angel beams some kind of psychic power upon the meditator. This externally originating power then produces the mystical effects, such as seeing bright light or feeling incredible peace and joy. Hence, mystical experiences depend on an external angel's willingness to act, rather than on the will, intention, or performance of the meditator.

Many New Agers sit in meditation for hours, hoping that they can reach a state of nirvana or bliss. Unless a satanic angel has a special motive in wanting to give them this kind of experience—such as to strengthen the meditators' faith—the poor meditators may well be sitting around for nothing.

Occult Meditation That Looks Christian

Under the influence of such books as Kelsy's *Guide to Christian Meditation,* many Christians are now engaging in meditation practices that appear to be very Christian in form and character.

When the Lighted Way became a counterfeit Christian group, our occult meditation ritual was abandoned, and instead we practised a meditation with imagery appearing to be quite Christian. For example, we simply visualized warm sunlight shining upon us as we imaged ourself seated in a beautiful garden.

Our instructions began: "Invite *Jesus Christ* into your garden. He is your protector from evil influences. Talk to him, speak to him of your needs, ask him anything your heart desires."

At the end of the meditation, we were encouraged to pray either the Lord's Prayer, or, alternatively, these words: "*Father,* I am your child. My name was written in the *Book of Life* before the foundations of the world were laid. Thank you, *Father,* in *Jesus'* name. Amen."

This ritual was very deceptive. The average Christian would probably find nothing seriously objectionable about the phrases used. Yet this meditation procedure was a product of Satan, designed to lead people into accepting the voice of masquerading demons as being the voice of the Holy Spirit. With this type of bogus devotional activity, the deceiver tries to lead even the elect astray.

Wolves in Sheep's Clothing

Satan's master plan of deception has now progressed to the stage where New Age "Christians" are openly announcing their intent to introduce New Age ideas into mainstream Christianity. The *Los Angeles Times* carried an interesting article that illustrates this trend.[1] The article reported on the Los Angeles Whole Life Expo, an annual New Age exhibition attended by 30,000 people. The report narrated comments made by Charles Thomas Cayce during lectures he gave at the expo. This churchgoing Methodist is the grandson of Edgar Cayce, the famous trance medium, who died in 1945.

According to the article, Cayce's organization, the Association for Research and Enlightenment, is "venturing into the far reaches of trance 'readings,' dream analysis and psychic phenomena. At the same time, it is introducing notions of reincarnation, natural health remedies and meditations to *Christians and Jews who do not want to sever their ties with mainline religion*" (emphasis supplied).

Charles Cayce is quoted as saying, "The people who are most interested are trying to keep a foot in both camps." Cayce holds a doctorate in child psychology. His grandfather, the medium Edgar Cayce—a Presbyterian elder and Sunday School teacher—was said to possess telepathy, clairvoyance, and precognition. Twice a day for over forty years, Cayce would lie down, enter into a trance, and engage in channeling the "Universal Christ Consciousness" to bring "useful" information to mankind.

Harmon H. Bro, a visiting lecturer to Harvard Divinity School, is writing a biography of Edgar Cayce. Bro is quoted as saying, "His [Cayce's] trance state was an extension of his prayer life." The book is "an attempt to re-embed him in church life and Biblical faith without ig-

---

1. Russell Chandler, The *Los Angeles Times*, February 25, 1989.

noring the fact that he took a reincarnation position as part of his material."

As you can suspect, the activities of Harmon Bro and the Association for Research and Enlightenment are very much a part of the subtle but profound New Age infiltration of the church.

One New Age book with channeled content has even found its way into some Christian circles. The multivolume, quasi-Christian *A Course in Miracles* purports to teach a procedure for changing people's lives and bringing them closer to God. Advertisements for this course have listed study groups held in various Christian churches.

A Course in Miracles was written by Helen Schucman, a Jewish psychology professor at Columbia University.[2] She claims that, beginning in 1965, she received the book's contents from Jesus Christ, who dictated the information into her inner mind as she wrote it down in a shorthand notebook. One may appropriately ask, if the book came from Jesus, why does it make several statements that are quite contrary to Scripture? For example, "The Son of God . . . is not Jesus but our combined Christ consciousness."

Even some mainstream Christian preachers are now stating that Jesus Christ was *not* God. Kenneth Copeland made the following statement while delivering a prophecy at a Dallas Victory Campaign.[3] The context of the narrative was supposedly the voice of Jesus speaking through Kenneth: "They crucified Me for claiming that I was God; I just claimed I walked with Him and that He was in Me. Hallelujah."

It is a tragedy that such a gifted Christian preacher appears to believe that a statement contradicting Scripture comes from a divine source. As I read Ken's

2. John White, "A Course in Miracles: Spiritual Wisdom for the New Age," *Science of Mind*, March 1986, pp. 10-14, 80-88.

3. Kenneth Copeland Ministries, *Voice of Victory*, February 1987.

"prophetic revelations," I'm reminded of the apostle Paul's warning given in Timothy: "The Spirit clearly says that in latter times some will abandon the faith and follow deceiving spirits and things taught by demons" (1 Timothy 4:1). I do hope and pray that Ken Copeland is not led astray by these deceiving spirits.

Sometimes we hear of other preachers claiming that God has spoken to them. How are we to respond to these claims?

I think we can only do as the Bereans did—test the message with Scripture. If the preacher states, "The Lord spoke to me," and then propounds some contrabiblical doctrine, he is obviously just as deceived as the New Age mystic who hears the so-called voice of God during a deep meditation state.

"Christian" Churches That Are New Age

Christian believers need to be aware that there are already many New Age "Christian" churches in existence that purport to be following Jesus Christ. For example, in southern California one group calls itself Christ Church Metaphysical. It looks like an ordinary Christian church: the pastor and choir members wear beautiful vestments; large paintings of Christ's Palestine ministry adorn the interior of the church; Christian hymns are sung during the Sunday morning worship hour. Unfortunately, on weekday evenings, classes are held in astrology, psychic development, tarot, Alice Bailey studies, and other New Age teachings.

Another church in my area of southern California—a branch of an international organization with headquarters in San Diego—calls itself Teaching of the Inner Christ. I once visited a spiritualist church called the Church of Truth and heard a visiting Episcopalian priest preach a sermon on the soon return of Maitreya the Christ. He was introduced as the former chaplain of the ocean liner *Queen Mary*. During his talk he often quoted from Alice Bailey's Djwhal Khul occult books and enthusiastically promoted the New Age teachings.

For a time, I listened to a nightly broadcast from a Christian radio station in Los Angeles. The first few times I listened to the program, I thought the speaker was a typical Christian preacher. Then one evening he talked about his conversion to *Christ* through a three-hour visitation *Jesus Christ* made to him in a vision. During subsequent broadcasts, I heard him openly preach New Age doctrines and talk about his affiliation with the New Age movement, describing visits to New Age functions during which he "fellowships" and "worships" with his Buddhist and Hindu brothers.

Several national church organizations also project a Christian image and do not use the term *New Age* in their vocabulary, but have teachings very much in line with New Age. I remember once attending a Unity worship service in a beautiful new church with about a two-hundred-member congregation present. The people looked like staunch, conservative Christians. Absolutely nothing occurred during the Sunday service to give any inkling that this was anything other than a regular Christian church. Yet, amazingly, if you were to study books on cults, you would find that the Unity School of Christianity teachings have their origin in the Hindu-based philosophies of Phineas Parkhurst Quimby, the man whose writings fathered the other mind-science organizations such as Christian Science, New Thought, and the Church of Religious Science.[4] These quasi-Christian organizations teach New Age doctrines such as reincarnation, and they generally advocate the practice of New Age–type introspective meditation.

Some of Satan's doctrines are remarkably deceptive, requiring clever intelligence in their formulation. When I first read the Alice Bailey books, I concluded that their contents were so sophisticated and appealing that it

---

4. Dr. Walter Martin, *Kingdom of the Cults*, Bethany House.

would have been impossible for any human to have written them.

It must be remembered that Satan was once Lucifer, the mighty angel in heaven. He and his angels were in the daily presence of God; thus they possess a great deal of divine knowledge. They now use this vast knowledge base to enhance the deceptive power of these apostate teachings. Because a certain portion of the New Age teachings are, no doubt, truthful—for example, some of the holistic health ideas—no wonder so many are drawn into Satan's trap.

Let us pray and earnestly study Scripture so we will be firmly anchored in the truth of God's Word.

Appendix 3

The Coming of the Antichrist

Is the New Age apostasy prophesied in the Bible? Can it be demonstrated that the New Age is the instrument that will prepare the way for the appearance of the Antichrist?

Benjamin Creme, a New Age leader and follower of the Alice Bailey teachings, in 1982 placed full-page advertisements in the world's leading newspapers. These announced that "the Christ" had returned, was living in London in a physical body, and would shortly reveal himself as the "Messiah" when conditions were favorable. Although Creme calls his *Christ* by the name of Maitreya, he claims he is the same person as the Jesus Christ crucified on the cross in Palestine 2,000 years ago.

On October 23, 1988, an interesting article connected with Benjamin Creme ran in the distinguished British newspaper the *Sunday Times*. The most profound part of the article, titled "Messiah Is Alive and Well and in London," read:

> A journalist from the Kenyan Times arrived. Job Mutungi also has a fantastic story to tell. In June he was present at a Nairobi prayer meeting of 6,000 people when a bright star appeared in the sky.

209

Shortly afterwards, a white-robed, bearded figure appeared, gave discourse for some minutes, then vanished. "Everybody in that meeting was unanimous that man was Christ," Mutungi told me.

On hearing of Benjamin Creme, Mutungi came straight to London to investigate. He brought with him a picture of the figure who appeared in Kenya. Pitchon[1] says it is the same man she saw in Brick Lane [London].

Another report stated that this appearance of *Christ* took place at the Church of Bethlehem in Nairobi.[2] If the reports are authentic, it sounds as if the Christian congregation was fooled into believing that the mysterious white-robed visitor was Jesus.

The Christian church has long held a belief that an Antichrist, masquerading as the Messiah, will appear in the world. Was this appearance of a white-robed man in Kenya an appearance of the Antichrist? Is Creme's London-residing Maitreya the same Antichrist?

The Antichrist in the Bible

The term *Antichrist* is found only in the epistles of John. For example, he writes: "Dear children, this is the last hour; and as you have heard that the antichrist is coming, even now many antichrists have come. This is how we know it is the last hour" (1 John 2:18).

John here confirms an existing prophesy in circulation among the Christians that an Antichrist would come. He further seems to differentiate this special Antichrist from other antichrists who had already come in his own day. Verse 22 tells us these were the liars who denied that Jesus was the Christ (the Messiah).

---

1. A woman who claims to have had a vision of Maitreya the Christ during a Creme lecture in 1982.
2. *Whole Life Times*, February 1989.

John understood that the coming of the Antichrist would be associated with the last hour, although he erroneously believed that the last hour had already arrived, a mis-conception Paul also expressed at one time.

In verse 27, John introduces the concept that antichrists are associated with some kind of counterfeit power, or anointing, and contrasts the real power of Jesus with a counterfeit power utilized by the Antichrist: "As [Jesus'] anointing teaches you about all things and as that anointing is real, not counterfeit . . . remain in him."

In 2 Thessalonians Paul gives a profound, clear prophecy concerning events just prior to the second coming of Jesus.

> Concerning the coming of our Lord Jesus Christ and our being gathered to him. . . . Don't let anyone deceive you in any way, for that day will not come until the rebellion occurs and the man of lawlessness is revealed, the man doomed to destruction (2 Thessalonians 2:1-3).

Paul is talking about a special person ("man of sin," KJV) who will be revealed during a great "rebellion" (an "apostasy" or falling away from the faith, NASB). Paul emphasizes that the coming of Jesus will not happen until the apostasy occurs and the man of lawlessness is revealed. Up to now, the Lord has not returned. Could this be because Paul's prophesy has yet to be fulfilled?

In verses 7 and 8, Paul talks about a restraint that will be taken out of the way "and then the lawless one will be revealed, whom the Lord Jesus will overthrow with the breath of his mouth and destroy by the splendor of his coming." Paul's prophesy obviously concerns events immediately before the time of our Lord's coming. It is thus very much concerned with the "last hour." Perhaps Paul's man of lawlessness and John's Antichrist are the same person.

The passage in Thessalonians next describes what this lawless man will do when he is revealed:

> He opposes and exalts himself over everything that is called God or is worshiped, and even sets himself up in God's temple, proclaiming himself to be God (2 Thessalonians 2:4).

Some theologians propose that this "temple" will literally be a new temple erected in Jerusalem. However, in First Corinthians, Paul talks about our bodies being *temples* of the Holy Spirit; hence the word does not necessarily mean a church building. If the Antichrist were to reveal himself in a new temple in Jerusalem, I think it would be obvious he was the Antichrist, and there would not be a successful deception as is prophesied. I believe the expression *God's temple* is symbolic of Christianity as a whole, the body of Christ, rather than referring to a specific church building.

Now, it would be unrealistic for the lawless one to claim to be the Father or the Holy Spirit. The man of lawlessness will therefore most likely reveal himself and claim to be Jesus Christ.

Paul used the Greek word *apokalipto* for "reveal." This verb means "to unveil in a supernatural manner." Luke uses this same word to describe Jesus' second coming (see Luke 17:30). This seems to indicate that the man of lawlessness will literally try to counterfeit Christ's coming, a view the church has long held about the Antichrist. We have a strong case that Paul's man of lawlessness and the Antichrist are indeed the same person.

Paul indicates that the power of the Antichrist is being restrained by someone, perhaps an angel or the Holy Spirit, until it is time for him to be revealed, no doubt the "last hour."

> The secret power of lawlessness is already at work; but the one who now holds it back will

continue to do so till he is taken out of the way
(2 Thessalonians 2:7).

Then Paul points out that the anointing behind the
coming of this lawless one is of Satan and that it
produces counterfeit miracles and signs. Perhaps it is
the same counterfeit anointing alluded to in 1 John
2:27.

> The coming of the lawless one will be in ac-
> cordance with the work of Satan displayed in all
> kinds of counterfeit miracles, signs and wonders,
> and in every sort of evil that deceives those who
> are perishing (2 Thessalonians 2:9, 10).

Some Protestant theologians believe that the man of
lawlessness symbolically represents the papacy, an
institution that took over God's temple (the Church) and
set up popes who issued decrees, claiming they spoke
with the full authority of God. Technically, the popes
claimed to speak on behalf of God when they spoke "ex-
cathedra," that is, "sat in their chair."

According to Paul, the lawless one is associated with
an apostasy. Is this aspect applicable to the papacy?

During the years A.D. 867 to 1048, the Vatican did
fall into great apostasy and evil. For example, Pope John
XII was "guilty of almost every crime; violated virgins
and widows, high and low; lived with his father's
mistress; made the Papal Palace a brothel; and was
killed while in the act of adultery by the woman's en-
raged husband."[3]

At the time Martin Luther started the Protestant
Reformation, Leo X was pope. He became an archbishop
at eight and a cardinal at thirteen. He bargained for the
papal chair, sold church honors, and appointed car-
dinals as young as seven. "Yet this voluptuary reaf-

---

3. Quoted from *Halley's Bible Handbook* (Regency/Zondervan),
p. 774.

firmed the Unam Sanctam, in which it is declared that every human being must be subject to the Roman pontiff for salvation. He issued indulgences[4] for stipulated fees; and declared burning of heretics a divine appointment."[5]

While Paul's prophesy that the lawless one is associated with an apostasy does in some respects have a parallel reference to the historical papacy, I doubt that this passage primarily refers to it. For one reason, the papacy did not generally manifest miracles, signs, and wonders. Second, the coming of the Antichrist is an event occurring at the last hour, whereas the papacy has existed for centuries.

Many biblical scholars now connect the Antichrist to the New Age and the "return" of its spirit leader called "the Christ" (Maitreya). Does this view fit Paul's prophesy?

Paul states that the impostor will set himself up in God's temple (not in Satan's temple). The term "God's temple" would infer a Christian institution. In contrast, Creme's Maitreya is a New Age *Christ* associated with a New Age institution. The Alice Bailey teachings say that the *Christ* of the New Age will *not* be a specifically Christian person, but rather a figure having the qualities of a politician, sociologist, and transreligious spiritual leader. Creme's channelings from "Maitreya" generally still corroborate this description.

The Creme/Bailey Maitreya is being "revealed" by New Agers in the arena of New Age occultism, hardly a fitting description for "God's temple." As Maitreya is being revealed in what is Satan's temple, he does not fit the prophecy that identifies the real Antichrist.

A more fitting background for the manifestation of the

---

4. The remission of punishment still due for a sin that has been sacramentally absolved.

5. *Ibid.*, p. 780.

real Antichrist is to be found in the work of the counterfeit Christian churches, such as the New Lighted Way. Their promotion of a false *Jesus Christ* is clearly designed to prepare for the Antichrist to be revealed in a Christian environment.

Let me review my experience at the Lighted Way after the mysterious visit by *Jesus Christ* to its director. Our metaphysical center converted into an organization claiming to be a Christian church. Its "gospel" message concerned the soon return of *Jesus Christ* to planet Earth.

We were taught that *Jesus* really was the only begotten Son of God, and he would imminently return to set up his kingdom, the thousand-year millennium. The spirits told us that *Jesus* would not return in quite the manner that the traditional church was teaching based on its "misunderstanding" of the Bible. We preached that *Jesus* would not appear in the sky with his hosts of angels and the sound of trumpets, but would appear in the world in a human form, possessing great charisma, power, and wisdom. We stated that ethereal cloudlike vapors might surround his feet, and this is what the Bible meant by the term *clouds.*

The description of this *Jesus Christ* sounds much more like that of a counterfeit *Jesus* destined to make his appearance in a *Christian* environment.

The Antichrist in the Book of Revelation

The Book of Revelation throws more light on Paul's Antichrist prophecy. John describes a two-horned beast that looks like a lamb but speaks like a dragon.

> I saw another beast, coming out of the earth. He had two horns like a lamb, but he spoke like a dragon. He exercised all the authority of the first beast *on his behalf* [in his presence, NASB] and made the earth and its inhabitants worship the first beast, whose fatal wound had been

healed (Revelation 13:11, 12, emphasis supplied).

In Scripture, a lamb symbolizes Christ, the slain sacrificial Lamb; a dragon symbolizes Satan (see Revelation 20:2). Hence this beast from the earth looks like Christ, but he speaks with the voice of Satan. Using his authority, he makes the inhabitants of the world worship the first beast. (For now, let's not worry about the identity of the first beast, a leopardlike animal having a fatal wound that was healed.)

To summarize the passage in 2 Thessalonians referred to above: the Antichrist will counterfeit Jesus Christ's coming (look like Christ), use power from Satan (speak from Satan), and will exalt himself over everything that is worshiped (will be in a position to command people to worship other things, such as the first beast). There appear to be significant parallels between 2 Thessalonians and Revelation 13.

Compare the next passage in Revelation with a similar passage in 2 Thessalonians:

REVELATION
"And he [the lamblike beast] performed great and miraculous signs, even causing fire to come down from heaven to earth in full view of men. Because of the signs . . . he deceived the inhabitants of the earth" (Revelation 13:13, 14).

2 THESSALONIANS
"The coming of the lawless one will be in accordance with the work of Satan displayed in all kinds of counterfeit miracles, signs and wonders, and in every sort of evil that deceives those who are perishing" (2 Thessalonians 2:9, 10).

The parallel is striking. The lamblike beast seems very much to symbolize the Antichrist. However, note that the symbolism may interchangeably apply to either the Antichrist in person, or to his institution. Verses 14 and 15 of Revelation 13 give additional information with which to identify the Antichrist.

> He ordered them [inhabitants of the earth] to set up an image in honor of the beast who was wounded by the sword and yet lived. He was given power to give breath to the image of the first beast, so that it could speak and cause all who refused to worship the image to be killed.

These verses tell us that the Antichrist (or the Antichrist institution) sets up some kind of image that is to be worshiped. Refusal to worship the image could result in death. Some theologians regard this image to be literally a great statue, or idol, that can speak and will command people to worship it. However, a speaking idol seems too obvious to be an effective deception directed toward contemporary Christians. More likely, "image of the first beast" is symbolic of something else.

Before we seek to clarify the identity of the "image of the first beast," let us now consider what the first beast itself symbolizes, that leopardlike animal that was wounded by the sword and subsequently healed.

There are differences of opinion among scholars. A common Protestant interpretation, the one I will focus upon, is that the leopard beast represents the papacy. As mentioned earlier, this institutionalized form of religion became corrupt and formed mutually beneficial allegiances with the political and economic powers ruling the civilized world in its day.[6] These alliances were used to enhance the papacy's ecclesiastical power. Dissent was supressed by force.

Please let my clarify here that I am *not* referring to individual Catholics. I am talking about the Catholic

---

6. See *Halley's Bible Handbook*, pp. 731-733, for a summary of the papacy's great apostasies, especially the brutality of the Inquisition periods.

Church as an institution. It is not for me to judge any individual person, Christian or otherwise. My consideration of the Catholic Church in the context of New Testament prophecy is concerned only with the papacy as an institution that promoted doctrines and practices at variance with Scripture.

Also, I do not wish to be dogmatic about the view I am about to present. As history unfolds, different interpretations may become evident. For now, I just ask you to study and consider this proposition.

Assuming the leopardlike beast represents the papacy, what could the image of the beast represent? I suggest that the "image" is a new false system of religion that in many ways is similar to (an image or copy of) the perverted system of religion symbolized by the first beast (the papacy). It is my proposal that this new, false system of religion will be "set up" by the infiltration of New Age, neo-pagan ideas into Christianity, just as the papacy was produced by the infiltration of ancient pagan ideas and secularism into the Roman church. The end result will be a perverted, New Age–oriented Christianity possessing the power and influence characteristic of the papacy during the Inquisition.

Historically, the power of the papacy remained supreme until the time the papal palace was moved to Avignon, France, in 1304. In 1798, the French dealt a crushing blow to the papacy when Napoleon's General Berthier arrested and incarcerated Pope Pius VI. Of this, the noted scholar Dr. Henry Halley wrote, "At the hands of Napoleon, the Papacy received its crowning humiliation, and loss of prestige, from which it has never recovered. He just about ended the Pope's political power in Europe."[7] Perhaps this was the "fatal wound" of verses 3 and 12.

If one accepts that the first beast is the papacy, it is

---

7. *Ibid.*, p. 279.

interesting that Revelation seems to predict that the Antichrist (or his institution) will promote people to once more worship the papacy: "He . . . made the earth and its inhabitants worship the first beast, whose fatal wound had been healed" (Revelation 13:12). This worship may not necessarily take the form of ritual worship aimed at the papacy and its pope. Rather it could involve giving special respect, honor, and status to the pope, perhaps as a result of extensive coverage and acclaim in the media.

Perhaps the "worship of the first beast" involves contrabiblical worship practices that are based upon the same practices as those instituted by the papacy, for example, the worship of idols. (In compiling its catechisms, the papacy removed the second commandment so as to allow idol worship in the form of veneration of statues of Mary, Jesus, and the saints.)

The papacy never abandoned Scripture; it just ignored, twisted, or superseded it to suit its own ends. This is exactly what is evident today in the counterfeit Christian arm of the New Age movement. It remains to be seen how the religious system produced by an amalgamation of New Age and Christianity will reach out to grasp political power and use that power to subvert the saints (those who remain faithful to Jesus) in an attempt to enforce contrabiblical teachings and worship practices. However, I do think this scenario of events could well be the "last-hour" events prophesied in Revelation 13:12-15.

Noted Christian authors such as Texe Marrs and Dave Hunt are already issuing warnings about the emergence of a dictatorial, United Nations–sponsored world government under the control of New Age philosophy.[8] Dave Hunt and T. A. McMahon's discoveries concerning the current infiltration of New Age

---

8. By Texe Marrs: *Dark Secrets of the New Age* (Crossway Books, 1987); and *Mystery Mark of the New Age* (Crossway Books, 1988). By Dave Hunt: *Peace, Prosperity and the Coming Holocaust* (Harvest House, 1983).

ideas into orthodox Christianity are especially illuminating.[9]

Though it sounds impossible that Satan's New Age–oriented philosophies can take over the Christian church, we do know for a fact that somehow Satan did manage to take over the institutionalized Catholic Church, converting it into a papal harlot that taught perverted doctrines while claiming authority of God. The Bible tells us that during end times, one of the main agencies causing the Antichrist church's rapid rise to power will be the display of "great and miraculous signs, even causing fire to come down from heaven." Whatever form these wondrous and miraculous signs take, they will no doubt reach their peak when the Antichrist appears in person and parades upon the earth with such power, deception, and charisma that many nominal Christians will proclaim him to be Christ. This will be the grand finale of the "powerful delusion" predicted in Thessalonians.

The Antichrist Appears to Nominal Christians

While the appearance of "Christ" at the Church of Bethlehem in Kenya is the first public church appearance by a mystical antichrist of which I am aware, I have been surprised by the number of "nominal" Christians reporting that they have been visited by Jesus. For example, while attending a camp meeting, I stayed in a rural motel. During a casual conversation with its manager, the woman told me that a year before, she had seen Jesus while on a solitary walk beside Lake Michigan. At that time, her daughter had recently died, and the woman was still in mourning. She reported that suddenly she saw Jesus sitting on a large log. He told her not to worry about her daughter because she was in heaven and was very happy there. Jesus then disappeared.

---

9. *The Seduction of Christianity* (Harvest House, 1985).

From my inquires, I learned that this woman was not a regular churchgoer. I asked myself, If the real Jesus had appeared to a nominal Christian, is it likely that this woman would have remained a nominal Christian? It didn't make sense. If the Jesus who sat on the log had been Christ, surely the woman would have been stimulated by the Holy Spirit into becoming an enthusiastic, churchgoing Christian. I had to conclude that this woman's *Jesus* was the Antichrist.

It is my suspicion that the Antichrist is privately appearing to many nominal Christians so that when he makes his grand appearance, a mass of people will recognize him as "Christ," and they will loudly proclaim: "The Lord is here! Christ has come!"

The fact that the Antichrist is apparently making private appearances to nominal Christians does not necessarily mean that the Lord's return is imminent. God decides when the Son of man will come, and God decides when the "one who now holds it [Antichrist] back . . . is taken out of the way" (2 Thessalonians 2:7). As Satan does not control the timing of these events, he has to be always prepared for his great opportunity to counterfeit Christ.

The book of Revelation describes how the Antichrist, or his institution, will force everyone to receive a mark on his hand or forehead so that a person cannot buy or sell unless he has this mark (see Revelation 13:16, 17). This mark, commonly known as the mark of the beast, is the name of the beast, or the number of its name (666). A description is given of what will happen to anyone who worships the beast and his image (the apostate system of religion) and receives his mark: "He, too, will drink of the wine of God's fury, which has been poured full strength into the cup of his wrath. He will be tormented with burning sulfur in the presence of the holy angels and of the Lamb" (Revelation 14:10).

The saints are not to worship the beast and its image, even though this causes them economic hardship and could result in death. The next passage extols the saints to endure and remain faithful: "This calls for patient endurance on the part of the saints who obey God's commandments and remain faithful to Jesus" (Revelation 14:12).

Because the apostasy and its revealing of the Antichrist will occur before "the coming of our Lord Jesus Christ and our being gathered to him," it appears that the saints will face some kind of tribulation prior to the Lord's coming and the gathering to him.

Paul explains why people will fall away and become in league with the Antichrist apostasy:

> They perish because they refused to love the truth and so be saved. For this reason God sends them a powerful delusion so that they will believe the lie and so that all will be condemned who have not believed the truth but have delighted in wickedness (2 Thessalonians 2:10-12).

The warning clearly indicates that the basis of belief and practice must be the truth as revealed in Scripture. Signs and wonders, tradition, prophesies, and new theologies are valid only if they harmonize with Scripture. "To the law and to the testimony! If they do not speak according to this word, it is because there is no light in them" (Isaiah 8:20, NKJV).

Who Is Lord Maitreya?

If the New Age Maitreya is not the real Antichrist, who is he? I submit that he is a decoy. Satan is very smart. Being a mastermind, he knows perfectly well that Christians are expecting the Antichrist to appear. So Satan has planned to provide one. In fact, it appears he has planned to provide several of them, just to add confusion. Maitreya is only one of them. The Reverend Sun Myung Moon of the Unification Church appears to be another. Moon says that when he was sixteen years old, he had a vision in which he was visited by Jesus Christ. Reverend Moon has since claimed that he himself is the one through whom the world will be saved. He is, of course, just another decoy Antichrist.

Satan's New Age seems to serve two functions. On the one hand it promotes apostasy within Christianity so as to prepare for the great deception in which many Christians (in name) will accept the Antichrist teachings as being divine truth. Concurrently, it provides a decoy Antichrist (Maitreya) to enhance that deception. Churches are led to brand Maitreya as the Antichrist, while the true Antichrist presence is developing within the church itself.

Overall, the master deceiver promotes two parallel operations. His angels incite crime, violence, drugs, pornography, political unrest, and every other kind of evil imaginable. Simultaneously, they cleverly promote and expand the world's counterfeit religions in an effort to seduce spiritually aspiring people away from God the Creator.

Finally, Satan will pull out his trump card. He will stage the appearance of the real Antichrist, a majestic being of dazzling charisma. Perhaps Satan himself will decide to masquerade as Christ. Whoever plays the role, this grand counterfeit will so closely resemble the real that only scriptural study will prevent deception. He will probably exhibit dramatic healing power and quote freely from the Bible, often repeating the words spoken by Christ in Palestine. The instigator of all the misery, sickness, and evil in the world now purports to be its savior in a crowning act of deception.

Christians who have previously seen *Jesus* will recognize their acquaintance and hail him as the Messiah. The devil's angels will work frantically to communicate to New Agers and Christians alike that *Jesus Christ*, the true *Christ*, has finally come to set up his kingdom, and all should bow down and worship him.

The evil angels will convince the Muslims that the

long-awaited Imam Mahdi has arrived; they will telepathically impress the Buddhists to believe that *Jesus Christ* is the fifth Buddha, and they will promote the Hindus to believe that *Jesus Christ* is the incarnation of Krishna. Satan finally achieves what he always wanted, to be openly worshiped as a god. "I will make myself like the Most High!"

All the world will fall down and worship him, except, of course, the saints. They will be patiently waiting for their deliverer. They know how Christ will come: "For as the lightening comes from the east and flashes to the west, so will be the coming of the Son of Man." "They will see the Son of Man coming on the clouds of the sky, with power and great glory" (Matthew 24:27, 30).

Speaking at the time of John the Revelator's apocalyptic vision, Jesus announced to the world, "Behold, I am coming soon! My reward is with me, and I will give to everyone according to what he has done" (Revelation 22:12).

Personal Acknowledgments

I would like to thank the staff of the Biola University Writer's Institute for their help in enabling the idea for this book to be turned into a viable manuscript. My special appreciation goes out to Susan Titus of Biola and Wightman Weese of Tyndale House Publishers for the very helpful suggestions and encouragement they gave me.

Last, I extend my thanks to all those who have been praying for me since the time I returned to the body of Christ. Especially I thank Pastor and Mrs. Siegfried Neuendorff of Redondo Beach for their kind support and encouragement at the time I exited from Satan's fold.